Hip Santa Cruz 6

*First-person Accounts of
the Hip Culture of Santa Cruz
in the 1960s, 1970s, and 1980s*

*Edited by T.Mike Walker
with the assistance of Ralph H. Abraham*

*Epigraph Books
Rhinebeck, New York*

For information contact:
Epigraph Publishing Service
22 East Market Street, Suite 304
Rhinebeck, New York 12572
www.epigraphPS.com

Book Design by Deb Shayne

ISBN 978-1-960090-05-8
Library of Congress Control Number: 2023902652

Bulk purchase discounts for educational or promotional purposes are available. Contact the publisher for more information.

CONTENTS

Preface

From Rock & Roll, Organic Revolutionaries, LSD, THC, DMT, Tipi tales & a Medicine Man's Tea recipe, the birth of Shakespeare Outdoor Stages, the UCSC Phd Thesis of Revolutionary philosopher-activist Huey P. Newton, and a Memorial for Paul Lee, co-creator of this series, this (perhaps) final volume of Hip Santa Cruz History presents a variety of voices. We started as a small circle of friends sharing psychedelic revelations and experiences. Volume 1 was printed in 2016, and we we have collected more than 90 stories for your enjoyment.

After several years of Drought, Pandemic shut-downs, insurrection politics, Climate Irruptions. Deaths, Atmospheric Rivers, floods & mudslides, the wrath of a wounded planet have conspired to slow us down, but not stop completely our determination to bring our inner & outer true memories and experiences forward for the interest, amusement, and cultural advancement of our community.

Thank you to all the writers, artists, photographers, scientists, midwives, musicians, shamans, dreamers, and fellow travelers in this adventure. Without you, there is no me. We are It: Life Itself in Motion. Telling stories.

Chapter 1: *The Dukes of Rock and Roll*
by *Phill Wagner*

My family moved from Watsonville to Santa Cruz in 1946. I was 4. Santa Cruz then was a sleepy retirement town with its curious, unique "seaside" energy. Fortunately for me, people who live near the ocean have a more liberal outlook than those who live inland. I was happy! Why? Maybe the two-piece bathing suits, the beach parties, the total luxury of just lying on the beach getting a suntan for free; reading a book, playing volleyball, going surfing, looking at the vast ocean, a far-horizon teasing out my imagination. At an earlier age, perhaps we beach-goers became aware of the vast possibilities of one another's bodies. We discovered we could purchase condoms at Town Clock Billiards or the United Cigar on Pacific Avenue. Birth control condoms were illegal in many states until 1965, Connecticut being the last state to ban them. Then for us, along came Chuck Berry, Jerry Lee Lewis, Little Richard and pulled the cork out of the bottle/ The genie was out of the magic lamp. Rock and roll was here to stay. Call it freedom. Call it individuation. Then in 1959, the birth control pill hit the scene. With that much freedom, you knew things were going to change. And they did. In 1960, you could purchase acid at the Hip Pocket Bookstore.

In the early 1950s outside Santa Cruz, paranoia still reigned with anticommunism, evangelism, the Red Scare, Senator Joe McCarthy, the eminent Atom Bomb attack, the Cold War, of course 101 religions with their endless scare tactics. But Santa Cruz, with the beach and Copper-toned bodies, seemed immune. Of course, yes, Santa Cruz had their fair share of fear-driven religions doing their fear mongering about devils and sins of the flesh, etc., but the Bible-Thumper's world view didn't find fertile ground with us because we already had our own "center point" experience of freedom. Something to do with "the beach".

Old Santa Cruz had a different sense of "time". Time wasn't necessarily for work; it was for going to the beach, reading, making music, dancing, speculating. We were the first young generation who had "time on our hands". We enjoyed "security", a sense of being loved by big mother nature. Earlier generations simply went to work on the farm ASAP. Politically, with the 1929 collapse of capitalism and WWII and the 50 million dead from a war promoted by the capitalist system fighting communism, the U.S. government wanted to make certain the country didn't turn to communism. Consequently, it encouraged unions, made credit available to average people and smalltime entrepreneurs, and did their best to encourage enterprise. They didn't want an anti-capitalist revolution. There were always decent jobs available. Teenagers could buy cars, houses, clothes, and be independent from their parents. We didn't need an economic revolution: we were past that, yet we looked for more freedom, a revolution in intelligence.

At age 18, I joined the teamsters and was a milkman. With my union wage, I could have purchased a house, started a family, and been the sole breadwinner for a wife and family of three. We had options. I went to college: it was affordable. In 1955, my girlfriend, Linda Adams', parents purchased a house on West Cliff Dr. overlooking Seabright beach for $30,000. (That same house just went on the market May, 2022, for $3,400,000). We loved the beach. Middle class people could afford a comfortable life. We were secure. Working 3 months at a union job in the summer, I could pay my way and go to a state university for 9 months. My parents paid college tuition. The University California Berkeley tuition was $280 per semester. As a group of teenagers, having basic security meant we could spread our wings and try new things, which we did.

It's part of human nature to have desires, seek fulfillment. I discovered playing music and dancing and started playing guitar at age 12. At age 14, I played in rock and roll bands. Repressed material could find its way into consciousness. I found myself a whole person. I first played with the Velvetones. Age 15, I joined by an old friend, Ed Penniman, in a band he recently formed called the Dukes of Rhythm and Blues. It was eye-opening to play on stage and "turn-on" a crowd of a couple hundred teenagers. Freedom uncorked! In 1957, our musical era began, but it should be taken in a larger historical context. We were an all-white band of middle class teenagers "crossing-over" into "black music". At that time, the "rock beat" was said by the Churches to (quote) "create a subtle confusion in the minds, wills, and emotions of the listeners, which leads them to question the absolute moral standards of God." The "blues" was "devil's music". We were teenagers, kids who were part of the first middle class that had ever existed in the world, forming an independent group outside the purview of our parents, our religions or our governments. We were the first teenage generation to own cars which enabled us to have privacy, "mobility", to be away from our parents, alone with our girlfriends to listen to whatever music we wanted, not church music! The black "Do-whop" sound and straight-up Blues music had a huge impact on us. It was our new lens on the world, our emotional lexicon. Cars had AM radios which were forever turned on to our favorite music station KDON. Music was emotional intelligence, corporal, a way of learning about ourselves and our own internal emotional, sensual, inspirational potential. Of course, we thrived in this "direct learning" from personal, unfiltered experience. We could be exposed to new ideas outside the classroom, create our own language of emotions, a semiotic language, and add our own forms of expression, essentially

"make history", not be "victims of history". Call it "freedom".
We could get "on stage" where we had "permission" to shine.

The Dukes would sometimes play with this other Rock
and Roll band named "The Downbeats." Their sax player, Joe
Serrano, would do the unheard of "revolutionary" thing of
cutting school in order to sit in his car and play his sax. He
was our hero.

WWI, the Great Depression, WWII, Korea, racism,
misogyny, the violence of poverty, etc., all of which are the
by-product of fear-driven set of rigid rules for thought and
action, indirectly promoted by self-serving institutions. It's
understandable: religions, governments, Wall Street, they all
have no authentic personal experience or center point and
thus are unstable, scared and "survival driven", locked in a
"winner-take-all", "zero-sum game" with the world. It's sad.
But with music, dance, the beach, good writers like Laurence
Durrell, D.H. Lawrence, Henry Miller, Theadore Roethke,
Allen Ginzberg, Kesey etc. we had a more stable personal
center point and didn't rely of group identity for security.
Kesey incidentally participated in LSD therapy at Stanford
University. A couple other people I knew also participated in
those LSD therapy sessions at Stanford and they too became
very successful.

Somehow we Santa Cruz kids of the 50s figured it out:
religions, governments, institutions in general, did not serve
humanity, they served themselves, primarily interested in
survival of their own parochial institution, their particular
ideology, their members, and not survival of humanity, any
"other" group, or what it is to be human. With WWI and
the Great Depression, the idea of "civilization" imploded.
Freud showed the world that binary, ideological, hierarchal,
repressive belief systems go septic: they become "human"
poison and irrupt in violence against "the other". But in Hip

Santa Cruz, the last thing we wanted were hard times, wars, prejudice, misogyny, classicism. My Santa Cruz generation was moving away from this religious mindset that projected its "dark side" onto the "out groups", non-conformists, misfits, the blacks, women (labeled "the handmaidens of the devil") or socialist-communists (labeled atheists "against god"). I went to Holy Cross Grammar and High school. Any kid who got too wild and free was looked at and branded as "possessed by the devil" and usually kicked out. Rock-and-roll was a form of "altered state" wherein the patriarchal judgmental world lost its dominance. This "altered state" didn't mean we were possessed by the devil, it meant we were releasing repressed material as part of a new healthy evolutionary process. As a bonus, we attained a new world view that wasn't black or white. The world became technicolor. "Love" was our god and our god was not exclusionary.

Our information and experience contradicted the "official story" of reality. My grandfather's family were all-Catholic for generations, but the World Wars destroyed the pretty picture of the Puritan, Edwardian family-political-social "Christian" structure. "Moral civilization" was irrational because the "morals" only applied to members of their group. In Santa Cruz, we weren't like that. In the old world, if you were outside the group-nation-religion, you had no defensible rights. You could be abused, invaded, colonized, enslaved, destroyed. After WWI, none of the waring nations could figure out why they had fought the war in the first place! A Catechism of black and white "morals" triggers inhuman action to "others". These "values" were so highly regarded and tightly interwoven, the wars just kept happening, and no one could say "no" to them or offer an alternative! There was no alternative point of view from an individuated person, that is to say, someone who wasn't indoctrinated by a religion, an ideology, a group-belief, a top-down patriarchal culture. When the nuns said "He sold his soul to the devil", it only meant that kid had individuated, differentiated from the religious mindset. He had experienced some altered state which allowed him an objective point of view on society's needless, cruel abjections of others which produced endless wars, pointless prejudice, and suffering. The kid with the new point of view, disentangled himself from the Parent-Child, top-down dyad.

In the run-up to the world wars, developmentally arrested, repressed populations flocked to volunteer to go to war. We Santa Cruz musicians all tried to avoid the draft. In the Viet Nam era, the government found that too many young people were refusing the draft. Why? Because that had experienced a higher view, they had gone through an "altered state". Richard Nixon declared Timothy Leary "the most dangerous man in the United States." The New Youth did not want whatever the old social structures had to offer. The publicized anti-human horrors of the Viet Nam war shook the foundation for any "cultural justification" and of "civilization" itself and its purported "values". Hip Santa Cruz was searching and finding a New Way. Individual nations narrow points of view and religions' accepted social structures were destroying the world. One trauma after another, families were being torn up. Information was manipulated to serve "the cause". As an example, in 1915 my grandfather, P.J. Freiermuth, had 9 siblings, but in 1919, he had 4; they suffered the loss of 5 children to the Spanish Flu. Why? Because for years the news of the flu was suppressed by the U.S. government "for the good of the country" because it would discourage soldiers and draftees from going into battle.

Like art and music, free expression in Santa Cruz presented an alternative lifestyle and an experience which built internal security. Korea and Vietnam mandated youth to look for alternatives. Post WWI saw young people trying desperately to get out of the puritanical Edwardian Era. The flappers, "speakeasies", jazz, and some "wildness" unveiled some humanness. "Enough with the brow-beating perfectionist authoritarians!" But then that generation was "reeled back in", repressed, with the Great Depression 1929-1940. Then WWII started and the State Department started their propaganda machines creating more repression. Religions in general were never really anti-Hitler. Religions were anti-atheists, anti-anarchists, anti-communist, anti-the free individual, a "non-believer" who was ipso facto, not a member of their "group". Post WWII, the Cold War began, with the perpetual threat of nuclear annihilation. "Moral values" were producing a world that nobody, except those authoritarian rich and powerful, wanted.

But in the midst of this Cold War, a middle class America had been born, and we teenagers benefited. We could purchase Fender electric guitars, drive cars, enjoy a world outside the admonishing eyes of the church, state, or parents, and we did. We endured the continual condemnation by fundamentalist religions. We persisted. As evidence in 1956, I recall an all Mexican band lead by a screaming sax player named Chuck Higgins which came to the Civic Auditorium. Fate! The teenagers went wild, "dancing indecently". Higgins had a hit tune, "Pachuko Hop", which galled authorities. The Santa Cruz Police Chief shut the dance down and the very next day rock-and-roll was banned from Santa Cruz. That cultural ban "for indecency" did not hold for long, but it reflected the basic thinking of the time, namely that, "people had to be trained, to be controllable and controlled at all times; they could not be free!" In 1958 the Dukes were playing a dance at Holy Cross Church Hall and the nuns kicked us offstage. "Couples were getting lewd, colliding and dancing too close, weakening their moral resolves." People out-of-control of the "authorities" were seen to be sinners, rock and roll was seen to break the laws of "common decency". Bill Kelly, a guitar-playing friend, was punched in the head by an offended member of the audience while singing some suggestive song on stage.

1957, a sexy woman was a vocalist in a club called "The Beachcomber" on Beach St. That bar was frequented by black bands and audiences which would come down on the "Sunliner" train from San Francisco. As it turned out, this sexy woman singing in the Beachcomber was discovered to be a transvestite. He was ordered to leave town or be arrested, essentially for violating codes of "common decency", which was a criminal offense. Ed Penniman and I, ages 16, used to go down and hang out in front of the Beachcomber Bar and listen through the door. We heard some mind-blowing great stuff. One time, a black band member saw Ed and I listening in and when they heard we were guitar players, they invited us up on stage to play a few chops with the band. I was too shy, but Ed got up there and performed. The band members loved us: two young whiteys digging the blues! 1958-60, TV Channel-11 organized dances at the TV studio and at the same Santa Cruz Civic Auditorium. The TV host liked the Dukes and tried to promote us. Our band, with two tenor saxes, actually sounded somewhat similar to the "indecent" 1956 Chuck Higgins Band, which was shut down at the Civic by the chief of police 1956. Music was a way of transmitting nationwide that dangerous "altered state" which made youth re-evaluate their existing society which produced so much needless suffering.

Music and the freedom it creates, is contagious. The Dukes could buy 78 and 45 records of groups from across the country. Chuck Berry, Jerry Lee Lewis, the Downbeats from Hollister and The Whalers. We played "sock-hops" in S.J.

at a kind of West Coast version of Philadelphia's "American Bandstand". We were broadcasting individual freedom: the right to be yourself and not a "member" of your parents' group. Teenagers were coming out, expressing themselves; suddenly they were not willing to be tied down to a counter-productive race-driven cultural form which was personally repressive, destroyed potentials, and started endless wars essentially to dominate people; wars to exploit weaker smaller childlike nations, wars to keep the citizens of their own country in line and "going to church", ironically justified in the name of "morals".

But rock and roll was here to stay!

I discovered the guitar when I was 12 years old and began lessons with Mr. Harder who owned the Music Box Music Store on Soquel Avenue. He talked me into buying a 1954 Les Paul Gold Top guitar and then a couple years later, a 1955 Fender Stratocaster. (Both guitars were first editions and are now worth $20-40,000). Later when I learned all the music I could from Mr. Harder, I studied with Jack Springer on Laurel St. He played guitar his entire life in Los Angeles. The first band I played with in 1955 was The Velvetones. Then I was invited to join The Dukes, who were more professional. They had two saxophones, two guitars, a trap set, base and piano … a much bigger sound. Ed Penniman was Stage Manager and Ted Templeman was the Business Manager. We were members of the Musicians' Union. The Dukes were something I could identify with: We were part of this larger social movement: a psychological revolution, far from traditional "group-identity" like church, state, and family, and moving toward a "personal identity" based on "connection", circumspection, non-violent non-racist tolerance, direct experience, and a broad cultural explosion wherein "pleasure" and "feeling good" were not sins. We created a "family of adventurous friends", all learning from interactive, immediate, and direct experience. We worshiped emotion, passion, sensuality, intuition, and dream; all the stuff of do-whop, the blues, and rock and roll. We were cross-over whites, although occasionally, Corny Bumpus, a black sax player (who later played with The Doobie Brothers and Steely Dan), sat in with us. The Dukes were basically a white band playing black music. Chuck Berry was "the father" of rock and roll and a kind of "father" to us. We loved Chuck's music, his energy, and other black bands, especially harmonica players like Muddy Waters. We adventured, totally digging the visiting bands, like Big Mama Thornton's, which performed at the Beachcomber Bar on Beach St.

Some of the local venues we played were: the Capitola Bowl, Holy Cross High School, Santa Cruz High School, the Coconut Grove (where once we opened for Conway Twitty), Santa Cruz Civic Auditorium, Channel 11-TV, Ben Lomond Riverside Park, Lompico Swimming Pool, and the Hollister Veterans Hall, opening there for a band we all looked up to called the Downbeats.

In about two years, The Downbeats, became very successful and so they packed up and headed to Los Angeles. In a couple years, they fell apart because of drugs. The lead singer, Johnny Armilo, became an evangelical minister in Salinas. The base player, Petey Rose, died of an overdose. The Dukes resolved to follow suit and go to were the music was happening, Los Angeles. I didn't go. Why? Because my father, in 1927-8, had traveled around the world in a dance band on a pleasure liner owned by Dollar Lines, and he knew firsthand the dangers of always being on the road, around alcohol, women and drugs. My dad told me flat out, "You are going to college, not Los Angeles!". Ed Penniman's dad told him the same thing, "You're going to college!" The re-populated Dukes of Rock and Roll left Santa Cruz for L.A., changed their name to The Tikis who had a sissy, white, beach-boy sound which I hated. It wasn't black; it wasn't rhythm and blues; it had no soul. The Tikis morphed into a stage band named Harper's Bizarre, which had a couple hits: "Feelin' Groovy," and "Chattanooga Choo Choo. " Harper's Bizarre was headed by our drummer, Ted Templeman, who later joined Warner Brothers Studios and produced the Doobie Brothers and Van Halen. Our piano player, Bill Davis, was super talented; he joined the navy and played in navy bands. Later, Bill also found success; he went big time, won many jazz awards, played with some wonderful bands and headed his own group, The Bill Davis Trio, which once opened for Ray Charles and an audience of 90,000 people.

The Dukes of Rock and Roll were part of the history of Santa Cruz and of a changing society. 1950-1970, music, writing, poetry, the Avant-guard nouvelle, art, new forms of psychoanalysis, all were beginning to open up. Santa Cruz was part of the change, moving society away from a closed society with "fear" as its prime motivation, fear generated by religions and governments for their own benefit. As a minor revolution, Hip Santa Cruz, was pushing toward an open, empathetic society, one that exists for the evolution of humanness.

References

Chuck Higgins
https://nickspicsblog.wordpress.com/tag/santa-cruz-civic-auditorium/, https://santacruzmah.org/2018/from-the-archives-santa-cruz-bans-rock-and-roll/,

Bill Davis
http://billdavistrio.com

Downbeats band
http://www.montereybaymusic.com/TheDownbeats

Ted Templeman
https://en.wikipedia.org/wiki/Ted_Templeman

Big Momma Thorton
https://www.youtube.com/watch?v=yoHDrzw-RPg

Paul Arthur Lee, Jr, PhD, 1931-2022
by Ralph Abraham

In Memoriam

For all of the books of this series, Paul Lee had a fundamental role, for inspiration, editorial guidance, and as a contributor to two volumes, #1 and #3. Sadly, he died before this volume reached completion.

We will remember him for his contributions to our Hip Santa Cruz History Projecrt from its beginnings in 2002, in addition to his many contributiions to the Santa Cruz community.

The early years

Paul was a superb writer, and regarding his move from the East Coast to Santa Cruz and his early years at UCSC, I can best quote from his chapters in this series.

In Volume #1 he contributed an autobiographical essay originally posted to his website, ecotopia.org, in 2005. Entitled *Oceans of Desire*, it appears as Ch. 7 of 25 pages.

> I remember the first time I saw Ralph Abraham. It was at a Faculty meeting in the fall of 1968. He was sitting in the front row. I did a doubletake as I walked by. I thought holy shit, they hired Abbie Hoffman; now they've gone too far! We were asked to lead a student protest against the regents who were making a visit to the campus. Reagan was governor. The Democratic convention police riot in Chicago had happened a few months before and the campus was a tinder box ready to explode. Ronnie and the regents were the match.
>
> I arrived for the march wearing my Harvard PhD robe, red silk with black bands, a representative

of lawful order and adult circumspection; Ralph showed up wearing an American flag shirt. We both had beards and Ralph had an afro out to there.

The students for the most part behaved but there were some outside agitators from Berkeley who acted as provocateurs and wanted to foment trouble. I invited the biggest loudmouth out into the parking lot but he declined.

Bill Moore, who was to become a graduate student in the History of Consciousness Program, had called for a Black Studies College in honor of Malcolm X and the Chancellor, McHenry, had laughed derisively at the suggestion. Bill was considered an inside agitator and was persona non grata for making speeches on the campus. In the middle of the ruckus he was removed from the campus by the police. I found out about it and picked him up at the bottom of the campus where he had been deposited and brought him back, where we were met by student supporters with whom we locked arms and marched into the Crown College courtyard. There, we were met by Rich Townsend, a student sympathetic to Moore's proposal, who told us that Jesse Unruh and a number of regents were waiting to talk to Bill. In we went to the Crown Library and Bill sat down to repeat his proposal, this time to sympathetic ears. Eventually, the X in Malcolm X was transposed to Oakes and a college devoted to Black Studies was instituted.

Ralph's and my picture appeared in many of the state newspapers in articles about the demonstration. Hate mail poured in. People didn't like professors with beards and they really didn't like their flag worn as a shirt. McHenry dutifully sent copies to us with a little red check on a tab on the side of the document. One of them suggested we fill our pockets with shit and lie down in front of a bus and become instantly embalmed. I thought that was an example of a rare imagination. Ralph had tenure and I didn't. I thought the jig was up for me and it turned out to be true, even though the Crown faculty gave me a vote of confidence at the time which was really a veiled kiss of death.

From Vol. 3. chapter 11, entitled *How to become a spiritual millionaire, when money is no object,* we learn from Paul more of his own understanding of his termination by UCSC.

The year was 1966. I had taken up teaching duties at the University of California, Santa Cruz, in a definite move to give my life a new direction. From Cambridge, Mass., to California. From Harvard and M.I.T., to a new campus of the University of California system, begun just a year before. I would own my own home. A swimming pool. The weather. The air. The vegetation. It was paradise. No snow. No freezing temperatures. Sub-tropical. The ocean. We thought we had lucked-out. And we had four more years to go before the tempestuous '60's came to an end. The hip 60's! Oh boy! Was Santa Cruz an epicenter for hip? Let me tell you.

Four years later, I had earned a sabbatical in Wisconsin, at our summer home, at Cisco Point, on North Twin Lake, where I could think about my future now that my present had come to an end. I had had a short shelf life at the university; it was pretty clear that I was going to be denied tenure, partly for starting an organic garden, the first at a university in the country, and pissing off my scientific colleagues at Crown College, because they thought 'organic' meant 'artificial synthesis', as in organic chemistry. They thought nothing of calling a factory a plant.

Our throwback, our practically medieval return, was the garden I started with Alan Chadwick, in 1967, eschewing the use of chemical fertilizers and pesticides; worse yet, it was seen as a hippie plot, devised to embarrass them further. That's what the scientists thought. After all, wasn't "flower power" one of the operative hip slogans of the time, identified with the hippie revolution. Organic schmamick. My career in teaching was on the line. The handwriting was on the wall.

After dismissal

Following dismissal from UCSC, Paul setup a writing studio in his garage, warmed by a wood stove. After my work day on UCSC's Science Hill, I would frequently stop there for a fireside chat on my way home. Over the many years he would try to instruct me in philosophy, reciting Greek writings from memory. When I began writing on cultural history around 1980 he would read my articles, suggesting improvements and supplemental ideas. This continued right up to the end, although my visits were infrequent after the arrival of the Covid-19 pandemic.

Conclusion

Paul deeply regretted his dismissal fom UCSC. He was a great lecturer, and longed to be in the classroom. The way things worked out was a loss for him, and a greater loss for UCSC. But also a gain for Santa Cruz, as he and Page Smith created wonderful structures for our community.

Letter from a Garden Variety Planet
by Jim Nelson

Hello dear reader!

I have been asked to contribute to the last volume of Hip Santa Cruz, edited by Ralph Abraham, an elder of the hip generation himself, and it is an honor to respond.

I grew up in the 60s, graduated in 63 from high school, and attended 4 years of college in engineering, mathematics, and, most importantly, literature at two of the campuses of the University of California.

Equally important was my appreciation of and immersion in the music of the 60s with artists like Woody Guthrie, Bob Dylan, Pete Seeger, Buffy Sainte-Marie, Phil Ochs, and Joni Mitchell.

I was in the audience at Carnegie Hall in New York in 1963 for Bob Dylan's first solo concert on that stage and at Town Hall for a series of concerts for "students and working class people" featuring, among others, the aforementioned artists.

Back in California at UC Riverside, I was influenced by the civil rights movement, and by my time in the Sierra Nevada in the light of the writings of John Muir and the early Sierra Club. In 1967, during the "Back to the Land" movement, I chanced upon Alan Chadwick at UC Santa Cruz.

Here is a piece I wrote about my two years I spent with Alan Chadwick and the influence they had on me.

1968 Dream of change, dream of peace, hope for love, hope for joyful work, beneficial work. A world gone insane, war and greed and consumption, assassinations. Change your mind, change your diet, change your heart, find a truthful and direct life, somehow go back to nature, remember and practice the lessons of wildness. Dream of change, marches, songs.

A young old man standing on a hillside eyes sparkling, hair tossed back, mischievous. Hands gesturing, working, holding life gently, showing us how to use our hands and our imagination, teaches about art, horticulture, fine foods, aromas. Learn techniques, tools, discipline, parties, picnics, hikes, learning, talking, observing while you work. (Pinch myself I am being transformed by my actions.) Get up at dawn with the light, sun sparkling on dew drops, birds singing the dawn chorus. I am just a part. Rocky hard soil, baccaris, broom, poison oak, roadcuts, dream, imagine, attend to details, work together, comradery, enliven the soil, the plants are as alive as you, the soil is our flesh, there's food to eat, beautiful vegetables you could hardly imagine. There is a heritage. Preserve the earth, save and simplify, but also nurture and enliven and create. Be careful, observe, use your hands and your mind and the hillside changes. Beautiful flowers and food and friends and we still had lizards and snakes, birds singing and bucket drinking air full of insects and sweet and earthy scents, work on problems, accept failures, sleep in the woods, don't worry about money or time, time is the moment pulsating with life. Reality can be touched and tasted and smelled in the garden, tired, sore bodies work to transform the nature of the university, integrate art and agriculture, science and humanity.

We have succeeded and failed, times are better and worse, people have had answers and solutions, finding and doing them all along. Change

yourselves until you outnumber the gray people,
wait and work, stay alive, find out what makes you
really alive. The next 25 years, it's harder now, but
maybe you've learned something, are wiser, more
experienced. Ripples have spread, roots and shoots
sprouting all over. Keep on working, remember
your teacher, your real teachers. So perhaps you
can be one. It's a small, fragile planet. Plants wild
and cultivated give us everything, our air, our food,
our shelter, our clothing and the beauty of a live,
pulsating planet. We need more gardens, more tree
planters, more people living simply. Creating and
transforming our place on earth and celebrating our
diverse society. The garden message is as vital today
as in 1968. More and more of us must sing its many
songs that we have learned and that have grown and
bloomed around our planet. We are stronger now
and how well we sing will create our future. Dream
of change, dream of peace, hope for love, hope for
joyful work, beneficial work.

My time at the Alan Chadwick Garden was
transformational and deeply felt. Here was a way to respond
to the challenges of our time with action, a way to be part of
the solution, a way to produce beautiful flowers and delicious
vegetables while at the same time making the soil more fertile
and the ecology more healthy.

At UCR and UCSC I completed 3 years of literary studies.
I was moved by the inspiration of poetry. The green pastoral
images of Dylan Thomas, the revolutionary spirit of William
Blake, the poems of Keats, Yeats, and Wordsworth. Then while
hiking on the upper campus of UCSC with Alan Chadwick,
he recited by memory The Song of the Wandering Aengus by

W.B. Yeats. I was at the right place at the right time; with my kind of people. The stanza that guides me most in my life is from John Keats' Ode to a Grecian Urn:

"Beauty is truth, truth beauty, — that is all
Ye know on earth, and all ye need to know."

Gardening and a Sense of Place

In the first year of UCSC, a visiting English poet, Donald Nicholl, gave a talk about achieving a "sense of place" on the beautiful land that was to become the University. During Q&A, he made three suggestions, one of which was to plant a garden. In the audience was Eugen Rosenstock-Huessy, a Dartmouth college professor and social philosopher who had fled Germany after the rise of the Nazis. With him was Freya von Moltke, widow of Helmuth James Graf von Moltke. The Moltkes were at the center of a German resistance group working and planning for a post-Third Reich democratic Germany. Helmuth was arrested by the Gestapo in 1944 and executed a year later.

In his "Letters to Freya 1939-1944" he asked her to establish a garden where young people could learn of "creation" as an antidote to the destruction of the world.

This coincides with Page Smith's belief in a moral equivalent to war and in the concept of the William James Camps where intellectuals could meet, discuss ideas, and do meaningful physical work together.

It was Freya who knew Alan Chadwick, knew of his ability to inspire young people (e.g. her sons), and of his commitment to ecological horticulture, to Rudolf Steiner's biodynamics, and to being able to start and found such a garden.

By good fortune, along with my first wife Beth Benjamin and my soon to be born first child, I had the opportunity to start my own organic farm a few doors up the road from Max Hartstein, a contributor to the first volume of this work. This was the beginning of Camp Joy Gardens, which is located in the beautiful Santa Cruz mountains and a home to a colorful and ever-evolving community of family, friends, volunteers, and a few special animals.

Thanks to Mina Jaff for her help in assembling this writing.

Die Before You Die: Sufi Saying
by T. Mike Walker

The first time I died was in 1944 when I was seven years old. We were living with grandma in Batavia, IL, while Dad was away at the war fighting Hitler. One morning I woke up with a fever and sore throat. I couldn't talk or swallow. Mom called a cab and rushed me to the nearest Hospital, Saint Andrews in Aurora, ten miles away. Same place I was born.

The Doctors recognized my problem — acute tonsillitis — and wheeled me straight to an operating room where I was stripped and put into a backwards gown — who ties a shirt in back? Then I was lying on a thinly padded table and they fit a mask tightly over my nose and mouth as a man's voice said, "Count backwards from ten to one."

As I started to count a horrible pungent smelling gas poured through the mask into my lungs and I couldn't remember if it was count 8 or 7 but "I" wasn't there anymore. Everything was Light, bright, and I was running from something over rough ground. With every step I could hear children crying, people howling in anguish, their cries coming from the very ground I was running on, every step was a shard of pain. I glanced back over my shoulder and saw that I was being chased by a huge lightning bolt, which kept stabbing me and laughing, and I cried out to It, "Why? Why me?"

And the Lightning bolt laughed again and said, "Why not? It's all You, Boy! This is the pain of the world! You're welcome!"

He stabbed me in the throat and the pain was so great I could only accept it, and then there was no more me, just an enormous silence that swallowed everything, and that was okay, I was at peace.

I woke up in a hospital bed and Mom was sitting next to

me with a small white bowl of vanilla ice-cream. "There you are Mikey-Boy. You were very brave and the Doctors said you didn't curse or anything, like most people do. He took out your very infected tonsil and said you'll be able to go home tomorrow. Uncle Archie is back on leave and he can give us a ride."

I told my mom about my experience between bites of ice-cream. When I finished she shook her head.

"Let it go, honey. It was just a bad dream. Everybody is having them now, with the war on everyone's mind."

I didn't argue, but I knew it wasn't a dream. I knew about dreams, but this one was as real as the ice-cream I was eating at the time. And the slightly bitter acid taste of ether made me never want to go to the hospital again. On the other hand, for the next few weeks I felt invulnerable. I remember bragging that I was Superman and God wouldn't hurt me and promptly jumped off the roof of Grandma's shed next to the cherry tree and broke my left arm.

So much for invulnerability!

The second time I died was in the Fall of 1953 when I started my Junior year at Mission High School, after getting kicked out of Balboa for cutting too many classes. It was six o'clock, a rare Friday night when Dad let me off work early so I could go on a date. I washed dishes, swept and mopped the floors, waited tables or counter, even cooked burgers and prepared lunch and dinner plates when needed every day after school until closing time at 9, as well as from 8AM to 5PM on Saturdays. I didn't mind. The Sip & Sup Coffee Shop on Hayes Street in Downtown San Francisco was Dad's big investment after getting his BA in Hotel and Restaurant Management from SF City College. We were three blocks from City Hall, so all the lawyers could hang out and play the pinball machines and talk shop with dad. We were also three blocks from the Opera House, The Museum of Modern Art and the Main Public Library. A kid could not ask for more! And Sip & Sup was our family kitchen where I ate three meals a day, even if I had to fix them myself.

"Be home before Midnight," Dad reminded me as I went out the door of the restaurant. "Remember, you have to clean the kitchen and sweep the deck before we open at eight."

"Right. No problem," I assured him, "The show lets out about ten, so I'll have plenty of time to walk Betty home and the buses run late on Mission Friday nights." I waved goodbye to my mom, who was waiting a table in the back. Dad was already cooking at the stove, a cigarette dangling from his lip, smoke curling up into his nose.

I grabbed a J Streetcar on Market and rode it to the end of the line at Church and 30th Street. It was only a few blocks from there across Mission and up the hill to Peralta Street where Betty lived with her mom and brother Jim. I knew Jim from Balboa High School and liked his sister, even though she was a year older than me and went to an all girl Catholic School — Saint Something — and she was studying hard, getting ready to graduate. She was hell bent for college and didn't have time to get involved with guys, but we hit it off and were just friends, enjoying some of the same books and movies. We were both sci-fi fans and looking forward to seeing *It Came From Outer Space*, playing that night at the Mission Theatre just a few blocks down the hill from her house.

Betty's Mom greeted me at the door when I knocked. "Oh, hi, Michael. Betty! He's here! That girl, always studying. You're lucky she's giving you time. She don't even eat with us some days. Oh, Jimmy's home from camp and should be here when you kids get back. He went out to buy a car, can you believe it?"

"Don't talk his leg off, Mom. You drive them all away!" Betty gave her mom a hug and kissed her on the cheek as she scooted out the door.

"Don't be late," Betty's Mom warned us. "We won't," I promised."Show's out by ten."

The walk down hill was brisk and it felt good walking with a girl, even if we didn't hold hands or make-out during the movie or anything like that. But we always discussed the movie afterwards on our way home, laughing a lot over obvious plots, bad acting, and stale popcorn. I loved her laugh and dark Gypsy eyes and we enjoyed the show.

On the way home, as we reached the front door of her house a small sporty black car pulled up to the curb and honked. A voice called, "Hey, come see my new car!"

"Jim!" We both shouted and rushed over.

Jim popped opened the passenger door so we could see inside the small compartment. "It's a '42 Dodge Coup, the last one they made before the war took over and they started making tanks. The guy gave me a deal."

The inside looked like the cockpit of an airplane, very compact and inviting with one seat straight across the front, and a thin space in back, enough room for a midget, maybe a middle size dog. "Hop in, Mike, I'll give you a ride home. Want to come along, Betty?"

"No thanks, Jim, you know me. Still studying," She turned back to the door. "Thanks for the show tonight, Mike. I'll see you around."

"Yeah. Thanks, Betty. See you later, Alligator."

"After a while, Crocodile," she laughed as she went inside.

"What is it with you two? You getting serious with my sister?" Jim demanded as I got into the car.

I held up my hands defensively. "No way, Jose. We're just

friends, fellow sci-fi fans," I explained. We just went to see
It Came From Outer Space. Where did this car come from,
man? It's way cool. Tight. Not like my dad's old Fords and
Plymouths or whatever weird brand he can scrounge cheap. I
like the smell of this one. Are the seats leather?"

"You bet, baby. $200 bucks right off a lot in Daly City this
morning. I've been looking for two weeks. Already drove
her at 90 half the length of the Great Highway this afternoon
when the Highway patrol was changing shifts and no one was
watching. She runs like a charm."

I felt a sigh of relief as Jim seemed to cool back down. He
always was a hothead. One good reason not to hang out with
him, since that's what sent him to Juvenile Detention in the
first place. Jim was strong and didn't mind punching folks
if he had to. He was always a friend to me and stood up for
me at Balboa a few times — that school crawled with rich
kid bullies and they all saw me as a target — which is why I
started cutting classes. I guess Jim had a hard time there too.
He sure wasn't rich, but he was tough and he was in great
shape, back from work-camp now and seemed to be in much
better control of himself.

I gave him a friendly punch on the arm, and he punched
me back. We both laughed. "Do you remember where I live,
Jim?"

"Yeah, down near Market street, near the Realto Pool Hall.
That place still there?"

"Don't know. My dad caught me in there one night and
kicked my ass all the way out the door down that long flight
of stairs In front of about a dozen Hells Angels who I thought
were my friends. They hooted and laughed and cheered for my
dad all the way because one of them owed me two bucks from
pool. I was winning"

Jim laughed. "Serves you right, Mike. Just because you're

tall doesn't mean you're old enough to be in there. Much as I hate to admit it, your dad did the right thing, Hey, before we go downtown, let me show you how smooth this baby rides, okay? You got a few minutes?"

"Sure, a few. Dad wants me home before midnight. I have to work early tomorrow around seven."

"You still mopping up your Dad's place and wiping plates? If you had a real job you could be driving one of these," H patted thee steering wheel.

"Don't want one. I'm just a Junior, Jim, and lucky to have a job at all. I just want to get through High School so I can get into College. Meanwhile, don't kid yourself. Washing dishes and hauling sticks of plates, peeling potatoes, hauling and opening five gallon cans of fruit and vegetables is exhausting. You can keep your Fire, I'll take hot water any time."

"Okay. So Shut the fucking door," Jim said. "Ever seen the other side of this hill?"

"Actually, no," I admitted.

"Check it out. This side gets the cheap view." He pulled onto the narrow street and followed it a few blocks until the houses ended and empty lots wrapped around the hill to give us a clear view of Hunters Point and the East Bay; further around and we could see the Bay Bridge and downtown. The Black Bay sparkled, reflecting lights from the Bay Bridge, the Ferry Building, and the Port of Oakland across the Bay. Several two story homes were under construction, cutting off the view.

We turned down the hill and headed out San Jose Avenue toward Daly City, They were building a new Freeway, Hwy, 280, to run along the coastal range up near Skyline Boulevard all the way to San Jose, but construction was still at early stages. I thought Jim was going to take us down 101 by the new International Airport they were still building near South San Francisco. Lots of kids I knew raced their cars down there.

The Highway Patrol didn't seem care, late at night when traffic was light.

Instead Jim turned on Highway One heading South, snaking along the coast. A full Moon sparkled off the ocean like dancing white light as I watched the miles go by and listened while Jim, told me about the CYA Ranger Camp in Boulder Creek where they trained every day to fight fires in Big Basin State Park, and eventually were trucked up to the Sierras near Tahoe to fight some fires up there. But mostly it was all in Santa Cruz, and on weekends they were allowed to go to the Boardwalk under supervision. His voice became a drone, putting me to sleep, and I finally rolled down the window and took deep breaths of the ocean air. "Beautiful! I love this world!" I shouted out the window.

"Don't shout, you asshole. Are you trying to get us busted?" Jim roared at me."I'm on probation, man. We've got open cans of beer In the car. One fuckup and I'm back in Juvvey, except I've over 18 so they'll send me to jail. Jesus, I forgot what a jerk you can be sometimes!"

"I'm sorry, Jim. I didn't know the situation. I thought I smelled beer when I got in."

"Never mind. Just keep your cool. Open a beer for me, will ya? They're in a case behind the seat. Open one for yourself if you want, You used to drink, right? What were you then, 14?"

"Fifteen," I corrected. "Tall at 14. Fifteen is when I started sneaking into nightclubs, wearing my Dad's suit. Heard some great Jazz that way. Dad would kill me if he found out."

"No shit," Jim laughed, gulping the beer. "Hey, did you see that Sign we passed? Santa Cruz 60 miles! That's near where the Forestry Camp was where they trained us. They've got a great Boardwalk there with all kinds of rides — Roller Coaster, Neptune's Grotto, a Tilt-A-Whirl, you name it! And the *girls* down there, Mike, you wouldn't believe them! They look so

Fine in their Bikinis out on the beach, you just want to eat them up! And they've got Surfing there, too. Looks like guys are walking on water, riding their waves."

"Sounds like paradise, but it must be closed by now. Oh my God — what time is it?"

"I don't know. Turn on the radio. They tell us the time every few minutes. Find us some good Pop music, Ragtime, Country, Pop…I don't give a tick.. Just not that classical shit."

I clicked on the radio, turned the bright green dial, and turned up the volume as I scanned the stations, getting snaps and squawks and lots of static because there was a wall of coastal mountains between us and civilization on the other side. Lights had been growing further in between and the last sign we had seen said Half Moon Bay 5 miles, and that was a while ago. Snatches of Mexican Mariachi music flew past our ears, then an announcer said in English. "…11:30 and our next request is from…" static.

I realized I was going to be late for my curfew, and we could never make it to Santa Cruz and back in time no matter what.

"Crap, Jim. My Dad is going to kill me! We've got to head back now. He's going to kick my ass and ground me and who knows what else as it is."

"Then what the fuck do you have to lose? Let's go to the Cruz."

"No! This is crazy, Jim..You've got to turn around and take me back. They're depending on me to be there tomorrow, don't you understand?"

"Okay, don't go ape-spit on me. I'll turn around when we get to the coast road where there's more room. Meanwhile, try and get that station back on. I liked the guy's voice."

We came through a long dark stretch of trees on a winding road that opened suddenly onto a stretch of clear road ahead with the full Moon bright above us. I remember glancing down at the dial as the radio squawked and then everything went blank.

The world turned dark and the Silence seemed to stretch like a giant yawn, enormous, comforting, spreading out from me in vast concentric rings. When my vision returned I found myself floating high above the ocean with the long sweep of the coastal hills stretching north and south as far as I could see, with the slender white line of Highway One snaking along the rugged ocean cliffs. Below me a mile long wave of black water formed, frothing white at the peak as it rushed toward the cliffs, churning in a long beautiful arch to explode against the cliffs in bursts of White froth.

But I couldn't hear anything? What was wrong?

I glanced up and suddenly noticed the stars — they were pulsing, they were alive, and I heard their faint whispering voices growing louder the more closely I listened to their unique voices and subtle tones and realized that they were singing, countless millions of voices filling space with songs, each different, each beautiful, all of them singing together, harmonies on top of harmonies, an uplifting ongoing song of praise and rejoicing beyond words, beyond beauty, lifting my heart as my mind soared with delight! The bright moon seemed to be inviting me to rise up and join them, to lift higher, to fly with them to wherever we were all going, and I was ready, but just before I let go of gravity I glanced down and saw, way below in a puddle of moonlight, a smoking pile of metal crashed against the cement barrier of a bridge across a pond which led to Hwy. 1. Hanging out of one of the car windows was a body, and a great feeling of compassion welled up in me, followed by a deep sadness, and I said out loud, *"Oh, those poor kids. They really fucked up!"*

And then *wham!*

I was back in my body of pain, staring down at a murky pond of water ten feet below me. My head felt like after my first (and last) football scrimmage when the whole senior varsity team kicked my ass to initiate me to the game. I never played again.

I suddenly realized where I was, what had happened, and what I needed to do.

"Jim?" I carefully pulled my head and shoulders back through the broken window. Shards of glass fell into the water and onto my lap. Jim didn't answer. He was leaning into the steering wheel, which had wrapped around both of his wrists and seemed to be holding him up. His eyes were open, staring straight ahead. He was breathing, but unconscious. I shook him. No response.

"Shit!" I shouted. I took a deep breath. "Calm down," I told myself. "Don't panic. Think! Figure this out." I realized that I was crouching on the car seat. Something solid but not the floor — the right front fender — was sticking into my seat and every widow in the car was broken. I remembered flying head first into the windshield and the loud "pop" when I bounced back out, only to hit the wing and door windows and then the back window as well. My face itched like crazy, but when I reached up to scratch, I cut my finger on a piece of glass sticking out of the corner of my eye. Glass was sticking out of my face and head like a pincushion. I dared not touch it anywhere.

Panicked, I started throwing empty Country Club cans out the window into the pond. Then I tossed out the rest of the case, about half a dozen unopened beers, along with the empty potato chip package and empty Pretzel box. I couldn't move Jim to get out through his door, so I cracked my door open just enough to wiggle out and climb up onto the crumpled car roof, That was when I noticed that the sole of my right shoe had been sliced completely off when the right front fender was pushed back up and through the floorboard, and jammed into my seat. I must have been flying through the front or back window when it cut through, or I would have lost at least one if not both of my legs.

No wonder they call it "The Suicide Seat"!

I could still limp on my right foot, so I started back up the road. Just before we crashed I had noticed a glint of light back in the trees as we flew past, and I hoped it might be a farmhouse. We were in luck, because the light was still on, lighting the path down a long dirt driveway where I knocked on the door.

Loud barking dogs greeted me from the other side and I heard voice shushing them. The door opened as the porch light blazed on. A little old lady was standing there, holding back a large dog with one hand. She looked at me, horrified. I must have been a site, a walking pincushion dripping blood on her doorstep. "I'm sorry to bother you, but we had a little accident down by the bridge and we need to use a phone to call for help"

Behind her I could see two big men coming toward us… and then I fell.

The next time my eyes opened I was lying on an ancient wicker bed on a screened back porch, covered with a fluffy white but bloodied quilt. Voices were approaching and two men wearing white scrubs walked in carrying a stretcher. I struggled to sit up.

"Hey, look at this, he's sitting up," the skinny older Paramedic quipped. "What about it, buddy? Think you can walk? It would make this a lit easier for us."

"I think I can. It's hard to walk on only one shoe, though." I struggled to get up and they helped me to my feet."

"Would you look at that?" The younger, heavyset medic said, looking at the shoe. "The sole was sliced clean off! I never seen that before. You were lucky it's not your foot!"

"No, please don't laugh. These are my Dad's shoes. He's going to kill me as it is." The older man helped me walk back through the house, where the family watched us leave.

"Thank you so much," I said as me went out the door. "I'm sorry for the inconvenience."

"Oh, Bosh," the old lady said. "We were just glad we could help. This is the third time this year we've had accidents down on that bridge. Just last month it was a Sheriff 's Deputy got killed! We need more signs there or something. Oh — my husband found your billfold with your Learner's Permit and address and phone number, He called your family and told them what happened. They were relieved to know. Your mother was so worried!." She smiled sweetly and shut the door behind us.

Jim was sitting on a bench in back of the Ambulance his wrists wrapped with bandages. He still looked shocked, but no wounds were visible. No blood. He nodded to me but didn't say a word all the way back on our hour long ride back over the hills to San Mateo's Emergency Hospital. But the old guy was talkative and stayed in the back with us while the other guy drove.

"So what happened, kid? That was quite a wreck back there. You were both lucky as hell to survive it. Car's a total wreck. Want to tell me about it?" The old guy leaned toward me, curious.

I glanced over at Jim, who shrugged indifferently and looked away. So I told the medic everything I could remember, except for the beer, just as I recorded above, including the silence and hanging in the air and the singing stars, the return to my body, climbing over the top of the car and finding the farmhouse. When I finished he sat there nodding his head for a few minutes in silence then patted me on the shoulder and said, "That's a great story, kid. You'll be telling this to your grandkids. You know, we handle people crashing and dying nearly every day, and I must have heard a hundred stories like yours — only all of them different, you understand? But really similar. Most of them see a Bright Light, or Jesus or Mary or their dead parents are there to meet them, and then suddenly they're back in their bodies again, ready for the next round. They even have a name for what you felt — they call it an 'Out of Body Experience'. I never had anything like it myself, but I believe you — I believe all of you, why would you lie? But you are one lucky kid, living through a wreck like that? Slicing off your shoe and all? — your case is definitely special. You must have someone on the other side looking out for you. With luck like yours, I bet you're going to live to be a very old man!"

When they wheeled me into the ER in a wheelchair I was shocked to see my father sitting on a bench smoking a cigarette. The clock on the wall said 3:30. Dad nodded to me as he stood up, snuffed out his cigarette in a sand container full of butts, and followed us down the hall to an operating room where my undershirt was cut off and I was stripped, wrapped in a gown that tied in the back, and told to lay down on the operating table, I glanced over at my Dad, who was holding his old shoe with it's sliced off sole, staring at it with a look of amazement.

After checking me over from head to toe — but mostly my head and face — one of the Doctor's said, "A few bruises, no broken bones, so that's on the plus side. On the other hand, you look like a pincushion, and you're lucky you didn't lose your right eye — in fact, you still might, but we're going to try to get that piece of glass out the corner of it without doing any further damage. IF we can, no promises. Now listen — we can't give you any anesthetics for this, we need you conscious while we remove the glass. Some of it is going to hurt, but your body is probably still in shock so you might not feel it at all. So take a deep breath..."

And Dad was standing beside me, holding my hand, wearing a sterile gown and a mask. He nodded to me and squeezed my hand every few minutes for the next hour while one by one they picked, pried, pulled and plucked dozens of smaller pieces of glass, but also over a dozen shards, especially around and into the edges of my right eye, which they cupped when they worked on it.

They never did get all the glass — tiny pieces kept extruding from my cheeks, my forehead, the edges of my eyes, and the top of my head for years. I started wearing my hair in a very short crew cut so I could find the damn little pieces as they appeared over time. But whenever one popped up it was a reminder of the most extraordinary experience of my life and the soul- lifting sound of the those singing stars.

The Third time I Died was in San Francisco when I was 27. This "death", however was proceeded by a series of "little" deaths — abrupt endings of life situations requiring dramatic changes through necessity, movement and chemistry, each of them leading up to a "letting go" moment of climax, surrender, change, adapting, and moving on. Briefly:

When I was 17 my family ran away from home — and me. They were in deep financial trouble with the restaurant and told me one day to quit school and get my transcripts together because we were moving back to Illinois and leaving Friday night after we closed. "It's the end of the month and we're only paid up to Friday. We'll leave the house keys in the landlords mailbox when we leave. Don't say a word, no forwarding address. Got it?" Mom did not look happy asking. Telling me? It felt like a trap.

I was shocked. I had not been paying attention. Things

must really be bad. But NO! I had a life, a plan — First, graduating in seven weeks from Mission High, the first school I ever loved, out of the fifteen others I had to transfer in and out of during our frequent "emergency" moves. I had friends and classes and teachers I loved. I already had the City College Class Schedule for this year so I could pick out the classes I wanted to take in the Fall, maybe even start reading some of the books from the class reading lists over the summer, find a subject I loved and then — who knew?

But return, go back, regress to Illinois? "No Fucking Way, Mom. I refuse to go. You can't make me, either. I'm too old. You can tie me up and throw me in the trunk, but I guarantee that the first time I'm out I'll be on my way back to San Francisco. This is my home, not back in Batavia where it's still 1925! You guys are crazy!"

We argued, we yelled and slammed around and made stupid threats to each other but not at work, only at home. So Friday after school I was tense, finishing up in the kitchen, anticipating another blow-out scene and wondering if I should just duck out the back door, screw the goodbyes. Back by the mop closet I had stashed an old suitcase packed with my clothes, plus my only heavy coat, an old sleeping bag from when I was a Boy Scout, and a bag full of sci-fi books I wanted to take with me but couldn't figure out how to carry. I was hoping to slip out and disappear before Dad returned from wherever he'd been. I was deciding how to lighten my load when Dad drove up in an old junker of a car about my age and parked it in front of the restaurant.

"Got you a portable bedroom and some gas money. Plenty of toilets around and showers at school or at the Y, Good luck, boy. You'll find out soon enough about more than you want to know. I didn't finish High School either, but you can't say I haven't provided for you. At least up to now. So here you go."

He handed me the keys to the car and $50 in small bills that
looked like he collected from Mom's tip jar. But I took it. I had
over a hundred in my pocket, saved from I don't know how
many weeks of salary at fifty cents an hour! I hoped it would
be enough.

"Goodbye, honey, I'm going to miss you," Mom said as
Dad turned out the lights of their dream and locked the front
door of the Sip & Sup Restaurant. He had already locked the
back door and we were standing in front of the building. I still
didn't know how or why this was happening, and it would take
years to find out.

Mom was shaking, on the verge of tears. She gave me a
big hug, then hurried up the street, towing my eight year old
brother Lou, who looked back at me and waved and shouted
something, I couldn't hear what, and when I looked around
again Dad was rushing after Mom. Their car was already
packed for the trip, parked in front of our rented Flat up the
block, with back rent due tonight. Dad helped Mom & Lou
into the front and the back, jumped behind the wheel, cranked
on the engine, turned on the lights, and with a honk as they
passed they turned the corner and were gone.

I never saw my Dad again.

So there I was, six weeks from graduation, standing in front
of the restaurant with a suitcase, seeping bag and books and
no place to go. So I loaded my suitcase and books into the
trunk, threw my sleeping bag and coat in the back street, and
climbed into my portable bedroom where I lived a few weeks,
moving the car — a 1937 Graham Nash — from place to place
around Dolores Park near Mission High, until the car threw a
rod on busy San Jose Avenue where I had to abandon it. I slept
a few nights in parks, always looking for a safe place, packing
my clothes around me for warmth, and finally couldn't take
it any longer and opened the trunk of a friend's car one night

and crawled inside, warm at last, even if a bit cramped!

"Ow!" I woke up the next morning as the car jack hit me in the head when we bounced over a curb. My legs flew out involuntarily and I kicked the back seat forward. The car stopped abruptly and the shocked faces of Ron and his Mother Clair looked over the front seat at me, their eyes wide with surprise..

"Mike Walker! What the hell are you doing in my trunk?"Ron demanded.

"Sleeping! It's too cold outside in the fog."

"Why aren't you home? Aren't you still going to school? Ron's mother looked so concerned.

"Yes, Mam. I mean, I'm still going to school. Just not living at home."

"But where's your family? Did you run away? What happened?"

"Well, see…my home sort of ran away from me…" I started to explain, and by the time I finished Clair told Ron to turn around, they would skip church that morning. We went back to their house and Clair fed me breakfast and set me up to sleep on their couch for the next two weeks, until I could find the next friend to stay with, and the next, as a small army of angels stepped forward to help me through graduation and beyond.

I found summer work as a pastry chef at a resort in Clear Lake, CA, then hitch hiked back to the City in September with some money for books in my pocket, in time to enroll at City College but again without a place to stay. Going on a hunch, I walked all the way to the home of Julie Olson, a girl I knew from school who had been in a Spotlight Club talent show with me and invited a bunch of us from the club over to celebrate after the show. Because this was at a time when I was always on the lookout for places to sleep, I had noticed an abandoned apartment downstairs on the lower floor, while the rest of the family — Tillie and Jack Olsen and their four daughters, lived in the two floors above.

I climbed the cement stairs up two flights to their door and knocked, wondering if I could rent the empty room. Tillie welcomed me into their home and informed me that the room had no back wall and no bathroom, so they couldn't rent it, but she urged me to stay for dinner so I could ask Jack and the girls when they came home from school. They all lived there too, and had a say in what happened And to my amazement we did discuss my plight around the dinner table. Julie was the first to suggest that I could use their downstairs bathroom if Carla would stop hogging it, and I suggested that I could hang a couple of big blankets up to cover the missing wall. It looked like the hole had been widened to eventually turn it into another room or a basement, but it had been abandoned many years ago.

Tillie had just won a Literary Prize and was a student at Stanford's Graduate Writing Program with several much younger writers like Jim Houston and Ken Kesey. Weekday mornings after they all left the house I would go upstairs to wash and use the toilet and eat breakfast at their kitchen table, and almost from the first day I would read Tillie's marked, discarded draft pages as she wrote her stories, learning how to write from reading how she cut and shifted and changed things around, always to clarify and make better sense. She would "discover" me as a writer one day when I asked her to read a short story about my break with my parents when they left me in the City. She loved it and said I had talent as a writer, and she offered to set me up at SF State after I finished my basics at SF City College. And one year later she introduced me to her teachers at SF State and told them to take good care of me and work me hard as she helped me enroll in the Creative Writing Program and practically paid my tuition by refusing a month's rent.

Soon after I married Kay Karpus, a dear friend from high school, who quickly became pregnant with our first daughter. Within a few years I was a San Francisco Policeman (*Voices From The Bottom of the World: A Policeman's Journal*, Grove Press 1970). When I graduated from college (Master of Language Arts plus a lifetime *Junior College, K-14 Teaching Credential*), but I was still working for the Police Department and by then I hated my job, my life, everything I was doing, all the pain I was creating, and I was facing a terrible divorce.

One night late I sat at my desk at home with the barrel of my police revolver in my mouth with the hammer cocked, ready to blow out my brains, when a voice in my head said: *'You don't have to actually die to change your life. Just die to all the things you're doing that you hate!'*

And a stunned silence fell over me like that time of the crash with the singing stars, and yes, that advice made sudden sense! There *were* other ways. All was not lost. I could change! I carefully lowered the hammer and put the gun back into its holster in my desk drawer.

My suicide was over. In a way it was a success because I started therapy, moved out of our house, quit my job as a policeman, and signed divorce papers. I thought I was starting a new life, but the old one still called me "Daddy!" and made sweet demands. I was separated from Kay, but not my daughters, who grounded me to our shared "reality".

After three years as an adjunct lecturer at SF State, they cut me loose because I wasn't pursuing graduate studies at UC or anywhere else. Just at the moment of panic, a long term substitute teaching Job for an entire year opened at Poly High School in San Francisco and I took it. (*RESPECT: Hippy High School in the Summer of Love*, Amazon on-line).

During this time, especially at SF State, I participated in an experiment in Creativity staged by the Psychology Department which had just received a shipment of LSD from Sandoz Labs in Sweden. They needed Creatives to test it on. They wanted to know if it helped or inhibited creative work. Did it enhance our creative powers or diminish them? Of course I volunteered.

And the answer was both yes and no in my case. Under the influence of acid I was totally passive, receptive, in a state of awe and wonder. It was only afterward that I could translate my new perceptions into words or, as it turned out later, into images that I painted, clipped, glued and turned into collage art pieces that sold much faster than my stories and poems over the next few years of experimenting with LSD, mescaline, Peyote, and psilocybin in a variety of locations and states of mind. I had many inner adventures and personal discoveries. Many of them were awesome inner journeys, although not always "good" trips.

Any trip you survive is a good one, as far as I'm concerned. Many layers of consciousness are messy to traverse, but the only way around these blocks seems to be through them. In all of these experiences I discovered many layers of the self, many little births and deaths, but there was always a "ME" experience/thinking/doing stuff. Every experience hinted at something more, deeper, truer to be known. Yet my insatiable thirst remained.

Shortly before I started teaching at Poly High School (09/67-06/68), one of my students from SF State suggested that I drop by his house for a treat, He didn't say what kind. We both lived in the Haight Ashbury District at the time and he shared the place with a dozen others in a grand old carriage house at the beginning of Golden Gate Park on Stanyan and Frederick Streets.

Al was just opening the door as I came around the corner and hailed him.

"Yo! Al! You called, I came."

"Oh, Hi, Mr. Walker. You're just in time. It was delivered last night."

"What was?"

"Your surprise! Ever heard of DMT?"

"Oh God, not anther drug! A few weeks ago I tried some STP and hated every minute, I was sick as shit and locked out of my body, struggling to get back in for ten hours!. If that's STP's high, I'd hate to see the low."

"No comparison, Mr. Walker. Not to worry," Al dismissed my concern as he led be back through a maze of hallways to a large space with Indian Music playing, sandalwood incense burning on a low table, and a large comfortable chair in the middle of the room. "This is our 'trip room' for meditation or whatever. Where we can be Holy and whole. Nobody bugs us in here out of respect, you know. This is Sacred Space, can you feel it?"

"Actually, I can. Like the back room of the Psychedelic Shop on Haight Street used to be before the Summer of Love dumped a million hippies onto Haight Street looking for a fix. Now it's just nuts."

"This isn't the Psychedelic Shop. We're not commercial here. I'm not knocking the Thelan brothers, because they are solid gold in their intentions. But money leaks in through all the cracks in the walls when you're a business. Look, do you have a few minutes to try our new doorway to God? DMT doesn't take long."

"Ha! I've heard that song before. How do you take it? Not needles, I hope. I hate needles."

"You smoke it, just like pot. You smoke pot, don't you? You take a puff or two and dream for about twenty minute and then you're back." He offered the pipe as I sat down in the chair, a bit apprehensive. "I'll be right here or in the room next door and can hear your every mood or sound, so don't worry. Anything goes weird and I'll be right here for you." He held the pipe to my mouth and lit the pinkish flakes of waxy material in the bowl. It crackled like resin when Al held the flame to the DMT and I inhaled the pungent, odd tasting smoke.

"When you breathe out, let go of T. Mike Walker," Al suggested.

It seemed like a good idea at the time, so I let go of it and took a second puff. The body relaxed as waves of colors and patterns pulsed around me, then beamed into my eyes; my forehead popped open like a third eye, vibrating like crazy until "I" suddenly disappeared. There was awareness, but it wasn't "mine", and as "I" started to panic it heard a voice say: *We got him,* as if "I" had been caught and was safe, and then the rebuilding began. I could hear molecules clicking into alignments, inner lesions healing, feel old wounds disappearing, all of it happening in a vast spreading peaceful silence. Suddenly I was shown a black soggy mass of something wet and pulsing — *"Your lungs,"* the voice said, *"Stop smoking tobacco or we can't help you further."* My heart cracked open and love flowed out and out, filling the universe, and this Love was alive, was *Life Itself* and it laughed and started signing *"IAM IAM IAM IAM IAM IAM" for what seemed like forever* and when I finally opened my out eyes again Al was standing next to me with a glass of water, which I drank in one swallow.

"You're back," he grinned.

"Who's back?"

"Ah! It worked, then. Welcome home, T. Mike Walker."

I looked around the room, stunned. "What the hell just

happened?"

"*Who* knows? He's the only that one that can tell and It's different every time for everyone I know who has smoked it. Nothing is ever quite the same again after DMT. Never quite so solid or dependable. Want to talk about it?"

"Impossible. I mean, everything was alive, in motion, changing, singing — did you know that the Universe sings? I think it's the stars doing it, like a Galactic Choir. I don't even have language for 99% of what went on — *what's still going on* in the universe every minute. And it's all alive and conscious and — holy shit! And..." I faltered. No more words would come. Here I was, a word man without words. There was no way to catch and keep all that with words, and memory wasn't built to hold all that information. But DMT was a switch that turned me on to it. I glanced over at Al, who was still grinning.

"So, that was twenty-five minutes by my clock. Do you want to take some home to try again later?" He asked. "We're just sharing it with friends for now. But were asking 25 for a chunk about the size of the tip of your little finger. You saw what just a few crumbs can do."

"It was like smoking 'Nirvana'. Thanks for the hit! And yes, give me the finger." We both laughed at my accidental pun as Al walked me back to the front door and put a waxy pink chunk of DMT in my hand.

"Here. Put this in your pipe and smoke it, Mr. Walker. You can pay me later. But remember, you can't step into the same *"Satori"* twice. Sometimes it's a sweet dream, other times it can be a smack to your head. Either way, you come back with new information. Enjoy!"

I did try DMT several more times, but Al was right. No two trips were ever alike, and on my final attempt I entered the Silence, the Darkness, felt the vibrations beginning, let go of T. Mike Walker, and that same whispering voice explained apologetically: *"There is no goal, there is no way. Next time you must get here on your own juice."* And when I came back into myself I knew this door was closed. They would only open when there was no T. Mike Walker to enter.

Back when I was seventeen scavenging for old Science Fiction Magazines like *Amazing Stories or Astounding Science Fiction*, a manager of the Civic Center Book Store on Market Street handed me a book on Buddhism. "This is one of the most Amazing stories you'll ever read, kid. It's only 50 cents., and much more interesting that science fiction. Check it out."

I was completely tired of religions. I had refused Baptism in Grandma's Church in Batavia — the whole thing bored me. In San Francisco I had attended two Catholic churches, and several different denominations of Christian sects — Methodists, Seventh Day Adventists, a few Black churches on Fillmore Street, a Christian Science Church and a Taoist Temple down in Chinatown where they also sold vegetarian mock-chicken and mock-pork food. Very strange, all of it.

They all claimed to have the 'truth', but not a single church resonated with me, although I did love the spirituals and the rocking congregations of the black churches in the Fillmore District. When I was in my Twenties and thirties I traveled to Mexico (many times!), France, Spain, Morocco, Algeria, Tunisia, Lebanon, Syria, India, Nepal, Pakistan, Afghanistan and Turkey, searching the Holy places for a sign. And I found signs everywhere, affirming that all Life is One, Interconnected, Indivisible, coming and going continually in an enormous upwelling of living creative genius and a vast and encompassing intelligence beyond words or imagination. Yes, our individual temporary lives are meaningful, which is why there is a here with "us" in it. So to speak. It's our challenge and our joy to help each other live long enough to

Know and Experience this ecstatic joy of Being.

I've had plenty of helpers along the way, both visible and invisible. Since that First 'death' (ego loss with pure experience), to the Second One when the older Paramedic in the ambulance assured me that I would probably live to be an old man because I survived that experience. And Now the writer spends many hours a day in silence, being Mindful and Loving and Friendly to All, following as many of Buddha's Percepts as possible. I'm still determined to "Open" under my own juice, as I was instructed. And there are many good moments every day.

Assuming Moments and Days exist!

As well as counting my many "deaths", I would also like to include my many "lives" in this incarnation, with its vast range of physical and emotional growths, entanglements, and karmic complications. From Baby Terry to Mikey Boy to Mike to T. Mike Walker are many seasons of still unfinished changes. You may be amused to note, for instance, that when I finished teaching that year at Poly High in San Francisco, I was hired by Cabrillo Community College in — wait for the rim-shot — *Santa Cruz, California-{death #2}*, where I finally got to the Boardwalk, and taught Writing and Literature for 30 years until I retired at 60, and where I still live today. I have been married five times with four children from three wives, and six grandchildren so far. If it turns out that they are all illusions, including 'me' and 'you' and everyone else, well…that's okay too. Because what is NOT an illusion is this ongoing miracle of Life Itself which all religions try to put a name and lock on. But no names or locks can fit. There is no "IT" to catch or get. The most important part of 'us' is already 'there', inside ourselves, if we would just slow down enough once in while to connect with our deepest self, which is NOT a name or particular form, but the whole damn wonderful thing itself, kicking and screaming, laughing and crying, living and dying, not just here but everywhere all at once forever.

Meanwhile, this body I'm wearing is 85 years old and routinely breaking down now, just as it was designed to do. Since our species seems to have been assigned an average expiration date of about 100 years, this writer is approximately 85% of the way through his "use by" capacity. Carl Jung advised that it was wise to know where we are along the progress of life's path, not so much that we should 'act our age', but to know where we have been, where we are now, and what we wish to accomplish in our futures, which allows for imagination and planning — two other things our species is good at!

So…what conclusions have I come to? None, since "I" haven't concluded yet. Still working on it. But some inner feeling has grown through the years, since that First peek through the door of Consciousness, until now, where "I" sit recording these memories, which come rushing through my mind linked together like railroad cars, each one loaded with a multitude of "Mes" from each decade, disappearing into the distance like clouds dissolving into the sky.

Not that I'm any hurry to leave "this Tavern of Drunken Souls," as the poet Rumi says. My personal train is still in motion. My Uber has not yet arrived. Time yet for another laugh, another drink, and lots of laughter and tears as we roll through the remaining days and nights of our singing stars!

!!!!

Interview with A San Pedro Cactus Medicine Man
by T. Mike Walker

I met Blind Jim in 1971 at the edge of the curb on Soquel Drive in front of Cabrillo Community College, where I was teaching Language Arts. Jim was a student in his mid-twenties who walked the hilly campus boldly, climbing the many stairs to buildings without a stumble or a guiding white cane or any external aid that I could see, in spite of his being totally blind. Which is why I was surprised see to him rocking back and forth on the curb in front of the College as a roar of traffic rushed past us. Many students randomly crossed the busy street to the lower campus, not bothering with the single crosswalk near the bus stop nearly a block to our left. But Jim was blind, and something seemed off with him, so I moved closer.

Half a block away I heard the hiss of the Watsonville-Santa Cruz Bus close. Jim's head snapped up and turned toward the bus which was picking up speed as it rushed toward us. His muscles tensed, as if he was preparing to launch himself in front of that bus — so I touched his arm and said quietly, "Don't do it."

Jim froze, turned, and seemed to look straight through me. "Oh, Hi, Mr. Walker," he said in a shaky voice. The bus woodshed past, on its way to Santa Cruz. We were both silent for a moment. "Thanks," he said. "How did you know my name?"

"Oh, I stand outside your group circles on the lawn and listen to your classes sometimes. I like that you encourage everyone to talk. Thanks for interrupting...I was in a dark place just then. I get these wild mood swings and just want to...well." He sighed, seemed to relax. "To tell the truth, my mom has cancer. She's a single parent and she's worried about me. I'm more worried about her, but she won't talk about it and I've been depressed for weeks."

"Can I walk you back up to the campus while we talk?" I asked. "It feels dangerous here at the edge of the road."

"No thanks, I know the way — I know all the shortcuts to get around campus. I even know how to get to your office. Why do you always leave your door open?"

"So my students don't feel shut out."

"And the pillows on the floor?"

"So they can be comfortable while they're visiting.. You're welcome to come in and talk or just relax any time."

"Even if I'm not your student?"

"Not a requirement. But I'll be in at ten tomorrow morning if you'd like to drop by and chat — or we could talk more today if you like?"

"Not now. Maybe sometime, though. I think you will be interesting to talk with." And without another word he turned and climbed back up the hill while I headed for the parking lot to steer my aging VW bus home.

Jim and I spoke often over the next few years but we lost touch after he finally graduated with over a hundred and fifty units and a major in General Studies. The next time I saw him was after he came into my office and told me he had found the stolen campus tipi cover — but that's a different story (which I'll tell later in The Coyote Tipi). What struck me most was Jim's bearing; confidence and authority oozed from his smile, diffusing the shifting of his unseeing eyes.

The canvas had been returned but I had a new mystery to solve — what had happened to shy Blind Jim that he could pull this off?

I called him and he invited me over to his house, down on The Flats of Rio Del Mar, which drained several Aptos creeks into Monterey Bay about another two blocks from Jim's two story stucco, Spanish style house set back from the street by sand gardens filled with dozens of flowering cacti, from small round green ones with spiky pink flowers to tall skinny San Pedro filled with needles, even a few Yucca. I followed the path around to a side door next to a tall solid fence that enclosed a large space behind the house.

"Mr. Walker!" Jim greeted me at the door, dressed in soft pajamas and a flowing red and black silk bathrobe. "Come on it, you're just in time for tea. Please leave your shoes outside." He turned to lead me inside while I slipped off my sandals and followed him in to his cave.

Jim wasn't born blind, His vision was normal until around four years of age when cataracts started growing over his eyes and he literally watched his vision fade. The last thing he remembers seeing with his eyes was the fuzzy red light of the tail-light of his dad's car. The Doctors scraped off the cataracts, but not the Glaucoma. Since then, his non-visual view of the world grew into one quite different from our own. His fingers and skin were micro-sensitive to textures and temperatures most of us never notice. Same for his ears, nose and taste, every sense heightened. Including a few extras. He can "see" inwardly and says his Spiritual teachers there have taught him many things.

Jim lives alone. Since his mother died he rents the upstairs to a retired nurse who helps with his housecleaning and shopping once a week and otherwise leaves him alone.

Yet a steady trickle of young men and women make their pilgrimages to visit him, seeking his advice and his tea — even the thieving brothers who stole the tipi cover! Jim assured me they were trying to reform, fighting their alcohol demons with San Pedro Medicine.

I followed his fuzzy bunny bedroom slippers across the plush white carpet that covered the cozy floor. A low ceiling and soft blue walls continued the cave impression in spite of two windows opening onto a side and back yard. But I remember again, that's where Jim lives — in darkness.

Back when we first met, he confessed that neither college nor things in the outer world attracted him. As he sifted through various fields of knowledge searching for the meaning of his life, he realized it was okay not to want to stock shelves at K-Mart or manage a Fortune 500 Company. After his mother died, his small inheritance and the deed to a paid for house permitted him to live modesty without working a 9-5 job. His Karma was special, but not without pain: his Glaucoma still drove him crazy.

Like many young people in the '60's & '70's, young Jimmy had sniffed, smoked, sipped, chewed & swallow every mind-altering herb, flower, fungi or chemical which came along holding promises, including LSD, mescaline, pot, mushrooms, peyote and Jimsonweed. In the process, he was told by his guides to stop all use of the truly dangerous mis-used drugs — alcohol, tobacco and Jimsonweed. He had even given up coffee for the tea he grew in his back yard. Blind Jim was a relentless explorer.

He was curious why I wanted to visit. I explained that his demeanor at our last meeting had impressed me and I wondered what happened. People don't often change that radically without cause, and I was curious. From this point on I'll mostly let Jim speak for himself.

"I was raised an atheist, and my mom said she was agnostic, which are religions of doubt. So I doubted — everything!

I guess I was looking for my soul. Some of the medicines gave me glimpses of Spirit, but others, like Jimsonweed and cocaine, tried to steal my spirit. For five years while my mom was in her worst pain, I was in a walking Jimsonweed coma. I went to school on it, did my shopping on it, rode the buses,

but all the time I was flying. I took massive overdoses to
see what it would do — sometimes as many as two caps of
powdered seeds a day. It was hard to urinate, but I wanted to
learn about the Jimson's *Die Now Live Later* program being
hustled by a smiling Assurance Salesman on the other side
who tried to convince me that it was all right to die, to go all
the way over, because life was eternal after all, wasn't it, so I
could always live again after if I wanted to. I was feeling very
suicidal then, very tempted, but I didn't sign the policy. I
thought Jimson might be my alai, but it was really my enemy
in disguise."

  We sat down on two plush chairs. Jim kept grinning, "I
know you're wondering how I got free from that Jimsonweed,
right? It was through the guidance of another plant!
Grandfather Peyote warned me away and convinced me to
Live now, that I'm Life Itself. He showed me the electric colors
of Existence. For a while Peyote was my favorite high. I'd buy
twenty fresh buttons for $10 and chew five a day for four days
and nights, then eat some more. I called it my four day run.
Peyote is for Indigenous and Coyote People. You can run
every day with it and not feel negative after-effects It gives one
an attitude of detached aloofness. I aways wondered, 'What
am I looking for?' Once I ate eighteen buttons in a single
sitting and there was an intense deepening of an inner state of
consciousness which sounded like a million Teletypes going
off at once. I felt like I was in touch with the Cosmic Telex.
After that I knew Jimsonweed was gone. Medicine Man Jim
was born.

  "About ten years ago the Indians stopped sending peyote
through when they found out white kids were abusing it,
making milk-shakes out of it and not treating it with respect.
Peyote is a Coyote Dog Teacher. It can be tricky, especially
if you're stupid like I was and try to combine it with alcohol,

because the two don't mix. Your Peyote Teacher will piss all over you to make a point if you fuck around!

"The Truth is, every medicine person has to pay a price for what we learn, We do things wrong in order to do them right; sometimes it costs us our life. Back at the beginning of my San Pedro Road I made a batch of juice that turned bad. I didn't know about sterilization then and I nearly died from drinking it. Then I herd a woman's voice calling from inside me: 'Jimmy, remember pasteurization!' It was the voice of a medicine teacher named Jill, who has helped me over the past four years. Nobody nows how the Incas did it, although I suspect they cooked other herbs with it for catalysts to boost the mescaline level. But which ones?

San Pedro is a very phallic, tubular plant that can grow over fifteen feet tall. Common in a million gardens and greenhouses throughout the south west. Its flesh varies in color from pale to deep green and it grows wild all the way down to the Andes where the Incas used it as a Medicine to treat insanity. You can still buy fresh bread-like slices of it in the Mercados near Cuzco. However, its recipes and rituals have been lost or hidden in the darkness of history. Who would guess that the ache of loneliness had driven this quiet, gentle blind man into a profound and intimate relationship with a ten foot tall cactus?

Jim claims he talks to his plants, that they answer back, and that the raw Spirit of San Pedro called out to him, chose him, taught him how to prepare and imbibe it, and gave him permission to reveal the recipe, along with some guidelines for its use.

"When I first tried chewing San Pedro at a party back in '84 it was very bitter, but I got a mild buzz from it and wanted to try more. A so-called friend said he could get some for me and sold me three two-foot sections for $50. Later I found out that I could buy it wholesale from a nursery, twenty pieces for $140, and have it delivered to my door wrapped up in newspaper because I have to deal with the needles myself. Would you like to see what I mean?" He stood up and pointed to a door opening onto his patio, so I followed him out.

A pile of three foot lengths of San Pedro were stacked like coed-wood against the outside wall of his apartment. He ran his hands lightly over their spiked stubble, touching each plant with loving concern. Over two dozen San Pedro cacti were alive and well, shooting up out of Jim's back garden like huge tubular erections, from eight to ten feet high. I had to ask the obvious question.

"So why do you keep buying the pre-cut cactus when you've got a garden full of them right here?"

Jim laughed and pointed to the cut stack. "These are my food. When I drink them I become one with the saints and their juice connects me with these living San Pedros in my garden, who are my friends and allies. They have individual names and personalities and they sing to me and tell me things about myself and others and the world around me. They serve as protection and emit a very high frequency whistle that keeps negative energy away. They give me instructions on how to improve my life and to help others. This is how they keep me on the San Pedro Road.

"Back when I first started sipping my brew the Spirit of San Pedro came to me and said, 'Stop complaining about the taste! You're drinking my blood, the blood of the universe!' So I learned to savor every sip. Another time I felt a massive splitting of my soul from my body as I was grafted onto the plant. It was creepy to suddenly feel a San Pedro cactus growing up inside me, but it was very positive, like being initiated and becoming one of the relatives — part of the family!!"

As he spoke, he wandered fearlessly between the spiked plants, pausing to pet them as if they were his children or loving friends ."Peyote and San Pedro have a lot in common, starting with their bitterness. But eating the raw plant of San Pedro doesn't get you off like peyote. It's not a fast drug or an easy one to use, even though you can buy it legally at any plant store or nursery. The mescaline content of San Pedro is classified as mild, but it can be concentrated by distilling because mescaline is very soluble in water, Back in '82 when I first found out that cooking it made it stronger, I started madly brewing up batches in my little kitchen, experimenting to perfect a process of purification.

"To make the brew, I first had to overcome a fear of hot liquids, because burning myself is always a very real concern. I went to the flea-market and found my most treasured tool — a stainless steel cooking pot that had been over-broiled and touched by chaos. Then, through trial and error, I learned how to remove the hundreds of needles from the plant, how to chop up the meat, how long to boil it and how much liquid to use. It's a very involved process, and to show my respect I make just as much of a ritual out of making it as I do out of taking it. It drinks me, even as I'm drinking it, and it has an earthy bitterness that I like. No one wants to drink anything that bitter today, but it produces a psychedelic high and gives me everything I ever wanted out of alcohol without the disastrous side-effects, It also stimulates visions and acts as a medicine to keep me from aging — do I look 37? Never mind, don't tell me!"

The fog had lifted while we were inside, and Jim flopped back on a patio chair and invited me to sit with him as we talked. He explained that rocking back and forth helped him triangulate sounds and other sensations and gave him greater depth perception. Tipping his head from side to side, he tracked the many neighborhood sounds that swirled around the patio like a light wind. The sound of waves breaking on the beach scarcely two blocks away, a motorcycle navigating the roundabout by the parking lot and roaring up the hill, buzzing bees and the fluttering of wings. Jim held up a finger for my attention and pointed to a bird on the tip of one of his San Pedro Guides. "That winged One comes to visit me every day. I know him by his call. I know he's a crow. He's like my brother. You know what I call him?"

"No. What?" Always the straight man.

"Jim:" He cracked up, cackling and laughing while the Crow cawed along with him, as if enjoying the joke. "I call all of them Jim. This one tells me about the weather and the kinds of trash he finds that we throw away"

A slight breeze brushed my cheek like a cool hand as I savored the flavors of the many sounds and smells of the patio. A clock inside on Jim's dresser announced: "It s Three O'clock."

"Time to go inside and start the ritual," Jim said. "I'm not so much a San Pedro Medicine Man as I am an explorer of our collective inner space. I don't believe in titles. I don't even believe in names, even my own — at least not as they relate to my true identity, which doesn't have a name because it isn't a thing. I'm just a person in the process of discovery, like everyone else. When I was a child I had lots of visions, but that's because I think all children are psychic, Death begins at adolescence. Adulthood is the real fall from Grace! Not since I was a kid have I ever had a vision without the aid of so-called drugs.

"Everything we eat or drink alters our consciousness in some way. San Pedro is very jealous and doesn't want me to come to Him with any other drug except these four — coffee, which I stopped using; pot, peyote, and tobacco, which I still use maybe once a year for a special Peyote ceremony I do with some Native American friends. They use tobacco in their ceremonies because it's their plant, it grows here. So does San Pedro. These are all natural Spirit foods if we use them correctly, which is to say consciously. They're not 12 Step escapist drugs that make us crazy. Alcohol and cocaine do that! They make you feel like you're throwing your life into a burning pit, but with San Pedro I always feel like I'm extending my life-time, getting more out of every second of my existence. With San Pedro I feel like I have enough. I Am Enough.

"The drug scene today has turned into cocaine, but it's all a big money hype, totally manufactured and unnatural. Cocaine is the white man's hell. I know. I got hooked on Coke because of tooth pain. I would rub it into my gums to numb them, but it was a false high. It attacks the hunger center and makes you feel like you'll never have enough of anything — sex, money, power! You just want more! These days they even have to use glue instead of ether to refine it because the chemicals are hard to get, and I worry they might start cutting it with other drugs.

"San Pedro is the opposite, it's a satisfaction doorway. It works on the pleasure and fulfillment center of the brain. Finally there is alcohol, which turns off the brain completely. I wonder how such a total tune-out can be legally sanctioned by society and allowed to produce such chaos? Who's idea was that? It's terribly addictive and dangerous stuff — it can even kill you with a simple overdose, yet it's the only drug our society lets us buy. It even permits manufacturers to advertise it and try to hook us on its use, yet it's the worst one of all!. So I don't feel so bad about what I'm doing. What could be more innocent than cactus and pure water?

"The first effect is the slowing down and lengthening of time, accompanied by a general clearing of sensory perceptions as all the filters fall away. Next there is a separation of body and soul, with a detached sense of happiness and unity. I finally know that I have enough. A kind of euphoric calm comes over me. The third stage is where memory stops and pure heightened experience absorbs me.

I can't describe the feelings. There is one more stage beyond where I have encountered a kind of a door with a doorkeeper who has refused to let me through when I had used alcohol during the previous week. This is how I learned.

"Back at the beginning of the path I went wild, boiling and drinking batch after batch for sixty days straight. I blasted right through that door into the Third World, which is a white man's hell that consists of a river of fire and the people in it are all in torment, burning up in alcohol and gasoline. But San Pedro carried me over that river in a big leap to the next realm on the other side This is the Fourth World, where the deer and bear, Indigenous people and other animals live, It's where their spirits went when they withdrew from this world after we killed them off. The Buffalo the Lions, the Eagles, they're all over there. Coyote controls the door to that world and if you're white you have to curse your own race to enter. Cats even have their own land over there. It's the place where we all came from, a kind of Eden. Every animal there has a medicine function. Bears, for instance, are great dreamers and they tend to stay in one area, while coyotes roam, running everywhere. But Bears have the power to appear in other forms as well — they are true dream creature and have very powerful medicine. A she-bear named Jill from that world is teaching me now, and she promises that I'll meet her someday here in the this world."

Jim tipped his head, as if listening, then called quietly, "Are you out there, Jill? Can you hear me? I'm ready!" He turned his face toward me, his eyes slighted crossed. "The truth is I'm horny as hell. Most of us Bears are Horney, especially in the spring when we come out of our caves." We both laughed.

"Alright, I'll tell you my recipe now. It took me five years of experimenting to Get it right. You need to assemble your equipment; the bowls and screens for straining the pulp, the funnels for pouring and the sterilized glass jars to seal it in when you're done cooking it.

"First, take the top two foot section of a ten to twenty foot San Pedro plant and remove the thorns. This is always a trip for me, since I can't see them. I get about one a month under a finger or thumb nail and go through hell unit someone helps me get it out. But that's part of my tariff, You have to pay in pain and blood and suffering for everything you gain. Nothing comes free in a Medicine Man's world!

"Next, peel off the outer skin and cut out most of the core — the fuzzy stuff in the center contains most of the strychnine, same as with peyote. I always leave a little bit of the ticker-kicker in there to act as a catalyst for the rest of it. A little of the skin is in there too, so you have the whole plant. Then I chop up the pulp and divide it into four cereal bowls.

You'll need one quart of purified water per bowl, plus an extra gallon because you have to add one cup of water every forty minutes while you simmer it with the lid off at a medium high temperature.

"Every two to three hours strain the pulp from the liquid through a fine mesh screen. Discard the pulp. Add the next bowl of cactus and a quart of fresh purified water to the remaining liquid and continue boiling.

"Repeat the process. Since it takes eight hours to brew one whole batch, I sometimes take a prayer break half way through and take two days to brew it. You get pretty high just from breathing the fumes while you're cooking it. "The distillation of four boilings from the four bowls of cactus increases the mescaline content of the liquid from about 12%, which is normal for fresh San Pedro, to about 48% potency. It only takes half a jar — about a pint — for a hit. But don't drink it hot. Let it cool to room temperature before drinking, or seal it carefully in sterilized jars for later use. I can't stress sterilization enough. After brewing, carefully wash out all pitchers, filters and screens with scalding water.

"I usually start drinking at two in the afternoon, There's no need to fast when you're taking San Pedro. In fact, it works better on a full stomach than an empty one because the digesting food helps absorb San Pedro into the blood faster. Sometimes I chew on a cinnamon stick to help with the flavor. I make a ritual out of it, one sip every eight minutes. It's more respectful to the spirit of the plant that way. By the time it come on, you're already there. The high is good for eight to ten hours of clarity, a rushing of energy, a feeling of strength, a true peak experience followed by two days of feeling drained and tired. Coming down is an important part of any trip, so it's important to have at least one day to recover and integrate what you learned before plunging back into the so-called 'normal' world again."

Jim gazed through the open garden door and sighed. His eyes slightly closed as he focused on some inner landscape. "I didn't know when I started down this path that I would be making my own medicine and sharing my path with others. By the way, did you know that Ram Das is living in Soquel? He came back from Hawaii and is recovering from his stroke, but he invited me over last month to share San Pedro with him. He liked it, too. Sometimes I feel like Sandoz in my kitchen, brewing my batches of psychedelic home brew. I'm like some weird New Age wine maker pioneering new dimensions, but what I'm doing isn't New Age at all, it's very Old Age from South America and Beyond. My brew creates a molecular binding of mescaline crystals to form a bridge between the outer and the inner worlds. San Pedro is a solid path which our ancestors walked long ago. I can feel it calling me like a drumbeat inside.

"I know there is always the risk of abuse, but the Saint told me to have faith and speak out. At first I was shy, but I've been reading Castaneda, and I realized that if Carlos can share his path, I guess I can share mine. Because San Pedro is the teacher, not me. These plants are intelligent, they're very psychic and can talk to us if we will listen. Sometimes I feel like the plant is speaking through me and I'm astonished by what I say — like today! Peyote and San Pedro speak to each other all the time in the spirit world.

"The Saint has given me some very strict guidance that I have to apply if I want to cross over. But following a Spirit Guide's rules has always been part of any path no matter which one you're on. Discipline paves the road to recovery and it's urgent for us to regain our health and sense of balance, because the Saint tells me that the Four Lights are growing weaker, the four sacred candles are going out, Maybe there's not much time left. I'm not sure exactly what it all means yet, but when I listen to the news on the police and sheriff's bands on my radio, it really sounds crazy out there. There's too much alcohol, too many guns, too much numbing of consciousness.

"Who knows, maybe San Pedro can help some people. It helped me and has helped a few others who I shared it with. What use is good medicine if you keep it to yourself? What about it, Mr. Walker. Are you ready for a cup of tea?"

Without another word, we clicked out cool jars of green tea together and took the first sip of the day.

Peyote Song
by T. Mike Walker

Spearheads of fire slicing your tongue
As you chew the beginning of time:
Bitter-root juices dissolving the self,
Innermost flavors of light.
Taste the earth and cry visions!
Drink the long rivers of night!
Sing the One Song of Silence, Knowing
That Love's your Lost Friend!
Grandfather Fire leaps with his hooves
Through a hole in the wood;
Black west metal melting,
Stars sucking heat-waves heavenward,
Shadowy tree shapes stirring the sky!
Leaf, stone, breath, bone,
Energy fucking and sighing:
Everything leans toward light;
Sky sparks falling, igniting the dawn:
The whole of the universe burns
In the bowl of this pipe.
All words turn into song,
Our prayers rise high with the smoke.
Hey! Hoka Hey Ya!
Water drums, rattles & clapping hands;
Moon dancing fire walkers circle the lodge
Wearing feathers of flame!
Thank you Earth Mother, you hold up our feet.
Thank you Sky Father, you carry our prayers.
Not for ourselves are we living,
Not for our personal gain does this beauty exist—
O, we are the children of Glory,

Cosmic creations of Conscious Light,
Burned beyond colors, races, age,
Our old skins falling away,
Our transparent wings unfolding
From the shell of our past
As crystalline new selves emerge,
Dancing our Dawn Selves Awake!

The Coyote Tipi:
Native American Literature in a Tipi Setting
by T. Mike Walker

1.

From 1972 to1986 Cabrillo County College was home
to one of the largest Indian Tipi's in California — at least
according to Goodwin & Cole, Tipi canvas makers in
Sacramento. Our 28 foot circumference request was the largest
they had ever made. It easily seated fifty people in a circle,
making it one of the largest classrooms on campus as well.
As a teaching tool, it was invaluable — a gift from the First
Class of American Indian Poetry and Prose class that dreamed
the tipi into existence and brought many Native American
Blessings to our campus — along with many surprises. And
problems.

In 1972 the Cabrillo campus was still new, but the
faculty and curriculum were rapidly growing every year to
accommodate a surging influx of newly graduated High
School students. Many of them were homegrown Surfers and
Hippies, Lots were Veterans returning from the Vietnam War.
Out of State students were arriving from Iran, Saudi Arabia,
Mexico and other countries. The Cabrillo Community College
student population was becoming deliciously diverse. So it
was no surprise that at our English Dept. meeting near the
end of the Spring semester Bill Grant, our Division Chair,
announced that the Ethnic Studies Committee had requested
a curriculum change for our Department to begin as soon as
possible: We had been given twelve additional transfer units
to our department to devote at least one class each semester in
Asian, Black, Chicano, and Native American Literature.

After a Heated discussion over who would or could teach
which subject, Joe Stroud, an excellent Poet himself, said

he would try teaching Native American Poetry during the summer. I was also teaching a special focus summer course (a four hour a day, four days a week intense focus for four weeks on one subject). Since I was investigating the Don Juan books of Carlos Castaneda, I volunteered to teach English 24, Native American Prose & Poetry that Fall. I was feeling close to the earth. My second wife had just given home birth to my third child, a boy. My daughters lived in San Francisco with my first wife. I drove up to the City from Santa Cruz to San Francisco every other Weekend to bring them down for a visit, then took them back up on Sunday afternoons. I know. Complicated.

Of course, that meant I had to create a Reading List for the course. Joe was focused on poetry, but I wanted to go with stories. As a published short story writer and novelist, I firmly believed that stories were the key to all literature, but I wasn't sure if that held true with Native Americans. The few Anthropologists and historians I had read didn't tell me anything about the People's Stories. I had already read Frank Waters' The Man Who Killed the Deer and Black Elk Speaks, but I wanted more, so I headed for Bookstore Santa Cruz where I met a friend from college who now taught Anthropology at San Jose State College. I told him what I was up to and a dark cloud crossed his face.

"Are you really serious about teaching about Indians?"

"Just the literature."

"Impossible. You can't separate the two. Believe me, I've been doing this for a few years." He glanced at his watch. "I don't have time today, but when can you give me about three hours of your time? I want to show you something important about the original people in Santa Cruz. It will change everything you know."

"I don't know shit" I admitted.

"Good Then you're open," he said. "Meet me in front of the

Catalyst at ten. Do you have a four wheel drive? No? Never mind, we'll take my Jeep."

The next day we drove North up US Highway 1 and turned right on Bonny Doon Road which climbed and forked and wound through redwoods until he turned off again onto a narrow unmarked dirt road that rolled over a tough old wooden bridge before we were blocked by a locked Gate after a hundred yards. No problem. My friend had a key. We drove through and paused while he closed and locked the gate behind us. "Part of the deal," he said, and explained more as we wound steadily upward.

For the next ten minutes it was all bump and grind, wind and climb as the jeep bucked us finally into a wide clearing blocked by an old eight foot high Industrial metal fence — and another locked gate that required a 2nd key, which my friend also had.

"This property used to be part of the old Tom Mix Ranch. Back in the Nineteen teens and twenties they filmed a lot of his Cowboy and Indian movies up here. It's been for sale for years, but a while back our Anthropology. Department wrangled a deal from the studio to allow a limited number of us to bring one or two graduate students up here to study some of the valuable archaeological sites. Especially the one called 'Squaw Camp' — God, I hate that name! Almost no-one knows about this place and our intent is to keep it that way. When you really start meeting the Indians, you'll know what I mean. There are just some things too precious to share. There is way too much Ignorance and disrespect in this world, as you know. That's why I brought you here."

"Thanks for your Faith in me on such short notice. But seriously — what's wrong with 'squaw'? Doesn't it mean 'woman'?"

"No. It's a very rude reference to a woman's vagina created

by French Traders. They could never get it through their
heads that in our cultures it's the women who are our Chiefs,
our decision makers, our Life itself! Excuse me, I go off
sometimes. I'm part Chumash myself, and only found out
when I asked my mom and she confessed her Grandmother
was Indigenous but never told anyone. Back then the State
paid you for every Indian scalp you brought in. No questions
asked."

He locked the second gate behind us, drove across a large
flat field toward a stand of trees, and parked facing the Pacific
Ocean, which we could glimpse through the high spiky tips of
a hundred redwood trees growing up from the canyon below.
To the right of our car was a long upthrust of sandstone that
formed a fifty foot high wall straight up, running the entire
length of meadow for about two football fields, ending in
a steep rugged understory crowded with manzanita brush,
Poison Oak, young redwoods and heavy vegetation. Nearby a
kind of ancient ladder had been cut into the cliff — hand and
foot holds carved into the wall centuries ago for people to get
to the top. But the first few holds had been damaged by time
or intention, and erosion had done the rest. This path up was
closed forever. I felt disappointed, but also relief.

"This way," my friend said, and I followed him away
from the wall into the stand of young redwoods. We moved
quickly along a narrow path between trees until our path
turned upwards. The trees gave way to a steep grade of hard
pack gravel and sand and suddenly we were leaning forward,
scrambling up a cliff that must have sloped 40 or 50 degrees.
To our left the Pacific Ocean stretched forever and far below
a thin slice of Highway 1 peeked through the canopy of trees
below. Of course there were no handholds, but we soon
scrambled over a ridge onto a long narrow plateau about 30
feet wide that ran the entire length of the wall we had seen

from below.

Pausing to catch my breath, I turned to look around and could see the sweep of the Pacific ocean from Pigeon Point Lighthouse 25 miles to the North, all the way to Monterey Bay and the Big Sur Range to the South, To my surprise there was an Island off Pigeon Point! I counted over a dozen freighters and container ships streaming up the route from LA to Oakland or Seattle. A wedge of Brown Pelicans many miles long streamed southward toward the upwelling balls of krill in the South part of Monterey Bay.

But most amazing sight of all was on the plateau itself. A dozen or more large grinding stones were arranged in small groups running about half the length of the Plateau. Some of the ancient stones were smaller, while others had been broken, I found an old bent pistol cartridge wedged under one of them. Here the native people crushed acorns to prepare their meals I suddenly realized the Indians knew how and what to cook, out of all the thousands of plants around us. The sense of my ignorance overwhelmed me for a moment. My friend said the women prepared acorn mush in hand-sewn leather pots, using hand made bone needles and hand-prepared sinew thread from the native animals they ate. Much further down was a circular depression dug into the earth. "This is where they held their sweats. You can see this was a holy place, a place of ritual and prayer."

"Except for the possibility of falling over the side, this was a safe place, hidden from Priests and predators alike. Nevertheless, a few drunken cowboys from the film studios came up here and shot up some grinding stones in the early 1920s. The rumor was that one of them got so drunk he pitched over the side into the parking lot below, which is why the Studio closed the whole thing down." My friend laughed. He looked at the shell casing I showed him. "Oh yeah. We

found lots of these, along with broken whiskey bottles as proof
of the desecration. Of course, we cleaned it all up as well as
we could and smudged the place to clear out the crazy vibes.
What do you think? Seen enough?"

I took a deep breath. "Can you ever see enough of this!"

"Good answer," he said. "Let's go back down."

On the ride back to town he said, "You could feel their
presence up there, right? Some of my grad students get
spooked, feel like it was haunted."

"I can see why, but it filled me with peace and — I don't
know what to call it — Open-ness? Awe?"

"That's what I was hoping for. Stay open, because now
that you're on the Red Road you'll be meeting some of the
People. Don't worry, they're going to show up, you'll see.
When they arrive, listen to them, They always have something
valuable to say about themselves that isn't in the books. In
fact, I guarantee it won't be in the books. Add *The Ohlone
Way* to your reading list along with *Tales of the Inland Whale*.
They're full of stories from California Indians. They lived in
a different universe from ours. Their lives revolved around
the stories they told each other. We do the same things, but
tell different stories. That's why I only bring a few people up
there, ones I hope can benefit from this glimpse into their
Indigenous spirits and will treat this planet and Native Peoples
with respect. It all starts with honoring our words and living
our Truths. That camp up there is one of the last relatively
unmolested sacred spaces left on the coast. The California
State Park System is planning to buy the land to preserve it,
but many of the Park Rangers don't even know about this spot,
which is okay. Some things should not be fucked with! Excuse
my French!"

We pulled up in front of the Catalyst. "Here's your car,
brother. Good luck with that class, because it's going to kick

you in the ass more than once before you're done. It did for me. But some of us can learn — If we listen." He gave me a thumbs up, drove away and I haven't seen him since.

So I taught the Carlos Castaneda Intersession class and talked to and arranged for a local herbalist to take me on a nature walk to identify local edible plants. She agreed to give a little talk to my Native American Literature students later in the semester. My good friend Fred McPherson, a Biology teacher from UCSC, took me on some river walks along the San Lorenzo, pointing out additional edible plants and the kinds of trees the Native People used to obtain the bark to shingle their semi-mobile homes. I had eight books on my reading list, which the book store complained were too many for the students to read or afford. I disagreed. This was advanced literature, after all. I had the whole 16 week semester nicely scheduled, each book marked with key passages to discuss, dates when each book analysis was due, as well as the mid-term and final exams.

Oh, the insanity of the anglo mind! Of course, none of it happened the way I planned — then or since

2.

On my way to Cabrillo on the First night of class, I rolled down the windows of my VW Van to breathe the fresh ocean air. It was a warm evening and the sun would be setting in half an hour. I realized that Native People on the coast lived most of their lives outdoors, and they got to enjoy natural sunrises and sunsets without guilt! When I got to school the parking lots were nearly full, and by the time I arrived at the small classroom I had been assigned, it was already overflowing, with every seat taken, people sitting on the floor and people outside waiting to get in. Only thirty were on the roll sheet but over sixty showed up, each with a pink slip signed by a counselor saying it was okay to admit them — but that would mean doubling the size of my class! On the other hand, students often signed up for classes and then dropped out later. Whatever happened, I couldn't turn away so many hopeful people.

I climbed onto the desk and looked around the room. "Hello everyone! I'm Mr. Walker, your Instructor. Obviously this room is not going to work for so many people, and I see how eager you are to learn about Native People. I am too. So here's what we're going to do. Tonight we are going to "go Native" as they say. I have lesson plans and book lists to pass out, but not enough for everyone. I'll need to run off more on the Department Xerox before I join you. If you are already enrolled in this class, take one each of the sheets and pass them on. I'll have more in a few minutes, and the books are available in the bookstore. I also have a set of the books put aside in the school Library for you to read there. Bookshop Santa Cruz sells most of them, so that part will be easy.

"For tonight, I'm going to ask you all to take a little walk up to the top of the hill behind the college where we can watch the sunset. That's what the Original People would do on such a nice night. On the left side of the upper parking lot behind this building there's a paved road leading up to the top of the hill, where there's a lone pepper tree that marks the spot where it's wide enough to sit in a circle and check out the view. Silence played a big part in Native People's understanding of Nature, so we'll start with silence and see where it takes us. I had a whole lecture planned for tonight, but this is not a normal class or a normal night and I am not a normal teacher, which will no doubt disappoint some of you, in which case the class will become smaller through self-selection. So I'm going to write a message on the blackboard now directing any late students to where we went and why and how to join us. Then

I'll run off these extra copies of the class schedule for the rest
of you. Do any of you know the place I'm talking about?"

Several hands were raised. "Okay, you can be the guides
tonight and show the others the way up. There's going to be a
full moon, in case you hadn't noticed, so there will be plenty
of light to get us up there and back safely. Are any of you
disabled?" To my relief, no one was. "Okay, follow your guides
and I'll catch up with you."

It was such a beautiful night! The road up was in good
repair and I noted a fairly large place on the side of the hill
below the water tower that might also be a good place to meet.
Near the top of the hill I was pleased to see that they had
formed a large circle with a slightly elevated empty place near
the tree waiting for me. I laid my large leather satchel filled
with papers and the class roster on the ground and sat cross-
legged on top of it, quietly settling in. It was already 7:30pm
and the sun was starting to set. A kind of hush settled over us,
and even the few stragglers who were chatting on their way up
settled down when they saw us and quietly joined the circle.

Meanwhile the sun silently did its lovely thing, showering
the bay with colors. Not a thread of fog in sight. When the
sun finally dropped below the edge of the world a flash of
green light caused many of us to inhale loudly all at once. I
had heard of the phenomena, but never seen it. Neither had
anyone else, so that started the conversation after probably
ten minutes of silence. I had never been quiet with that many
people before in a school classroom, and as I passed around
the additional reading lists, etc., I laughed out loud. "Now *this*
is a classroom that fits us," I exclaimed.

"Until it rains," one of the women pointed out.

"Good thing we're not Indians," someone else said. "We
have enough sense to go inside. Don't we?"

After a moment another woman said, "Wouldn't it be nice

to have our own tipi to wrap around us? We could have a fire when it got cold, and lift it's skirts on a hot day to let in the air."

"I'm all for lifting skirts," one of the guys said, and uneasy laughter moved around the circle.

"It's okay to laugh in this class," I assured them. "I've been told that Native People are always joking around making fun of us and each other. You'll see that in the stories we'll be reading. In fact, some of them are downright Bawdy, as you'll see in *The Daughters of Copper Woman* — one of the most powerful examples of Indigenous women in action.

"We're here to discuss the stories and books and find out what they have to say about the First People, and also about us in comparison. Remember, 'Indians' where then and are still fully human beings, every bit as conscious and intelligent as we are. They just knew and believed different things than our own ancestors from Europe, who proceeded to murder and enslave almost a whole continent full of people who disagreed with them. It wasn't superior philosophy that conquered the First People, but Greed and a superior technology. Guns and racist Christianity were the final blows to them collectively, although many of their cultures and beliefs continue today within the remaining fragments of their tribes. Remember, we are reading the stories of real People, not the imaginary creatures Hollywood created through countless movies, books, and lies. Let's begin with curiosity, open hearts and open minds. And I promise you, this will probably be my longest speech of the semester, because I expect each of you to come to class with questions prompted by your readings.

"Next week we'll meet at the assigned classroom and walk over to where-ever a bigger room is that I can get assigned to us. I'm open to a class discussion about getting a tipi and all that might require. Meanwhile, let's enjoy the books as much as I hope you enjoyed tonight's sunset. The first book we'll discuss will be *The Ohlone Way*, and I'll know by then if I can admit the rest of you to into the class. If you want a grade, you'll have to write all the papers and take the tests. Otherwise you can opt to take the course for Credit without a grade, just like at the University. The class will count for your units, but not affect your GPA, which I know some of you are worried about. Please watch your steps and help each other down the road to the campus. Goodnight." I followed them back down to our cars and drove home, excited and terrified about what was to come.

No larger classrooms were available at the time of my next evening class, so I arranged with Billy Paul, the Student Activities coordinator, to use the large student meeting room which adjoined the cafeteria, separated by a fifty foot long curtain we could close for privacy, while a wall of floor-to-ceiling windows looked out on Monterey Bay to the West. A Great room!

We had to shift the heavy couches, chairs and tables to form a kind of oblong instead of a circle, but there were half a dozen fewer students the second night, and I admitted everyone else on the waiting list. We spent the first hour discussing *The Ohlone Way*, when one of the students named Lodge Owl (yes, his official name!) said he knew Michael Harney, who did the illustrations for *The Ohlone Way*, and he had met Malcolm Margolin the author though a local artist named Daniel Stolpe who just moved to town. He offered to take me to meet Stolpe later in the week. It was like my Anthropologist friend had advised: "The People will come to you — pay attention!"

Lodge Owl was a crossbreed between his German father and his Native mother who was a recognized member of the Amah Mutson tribe from the Watsonville area. He volunteered to lead a small committee to research tipis and find out what it would take to construct one on campus. By the third meeting we learned that we could not sew our own canvas, since the college did not have any industrial sewing machines with needles heavy enough to penetrate canvas. He gave me the name of a tipi maker, Goodwin & Cole out of Sacramento, and we called them to inquire.

Given the number of people we needed to fit inside, the company said they had never made a lodge large enough to contain 50 people. The base would be 32 feet in diameter and rise to 28 feet, and the poles would need to be at least 35 feet long. The biggest "skin" they made commercially was 24 feet. They could make one the size we needed, using 10 oz 'Duck' canvas, but they didn't have tipi poles long enough for the frame. We would have to find, harvest, and prepare our own poles. They could stitch the outer 'skin', adding the door cover, sewn button holes, and 50 feet of 3/8" rope, plus Flame Retardant treatment for around $700. A floor would cost an additional $300 more and a liner $250 more. Over $1,000. But we would have to create our own skeleton for the skin.

When this was explained to the class, two dozen students volunteered to cut down, haul, trim, strip, and paint the poles with water-sealer themselves if the rest of us could figure out how to raise money for the cover. They decided we didn't need a floor, and the liner could wait.

I had to stop the discussion at this point to explain that we could not cut any of the trees on campus. Second, fresh cut trees that long were enormously heavy and dangerous to mess with. Also damn near impossible to move without a long-bed truck like PG&E used to haul telephone poles. Of all the students, only Lodge Owl had ever done such work before, but the group was determined to move forward. Lodge Owl agreed to help and suggested that we might find what we needed behind his family property far back in the Soquel hills.

Over a dozen students volunteered and I raised my own hand, agreeing to join them. On or off campus, I was going to be responsible for this project, so I resolved to be active.

Lodge Owl told us they had dozens of redwood saplings on his property that had been crowded out by the larger trees. The small ones had died and dried out while still standing and were waiting for the next storm to blow them over. He had used some of these for his own tipi and felt sure they would work for us if we could find enough. But his elders had taught him that certain rituals, prayers and offerings must be made first. A red tobacco tie containing special herbs had to be offered to each tree we take, along with our prayers for it, explaining why we needed it and how it would be used for good. During the next class he brought in the herbs and tobacco for the tree cullers and we spent the last hour rolling up our offerings for 19 poles as we continued discussing the stories in *Tales of The Inland Whale* while the rest of the class planned fund-raising strategies. Half a dozen formed a club called Friends of the Tipi and joined the student council where they could apply for funds to help our project.

That Saturday our caravan of half a dozen cars followed Lodge Owl and me, driving Cabrillo's large flat bed truck down Rodeo Gulch Road for miles, past Lodge Owl's family farm in the Soquel hills to their overgrown back grove of Redwoods. For the next three hours we trekked through the woods measuring dead trees and toppling them by not-so-gently pushing them over. All but one fell perfectly without breaking. The broken one left us one pole short, and we couldn't find another, so we dragged what we had down to the truck and loaded them on.

Four of our party still hadn't returned when we heard a terrible crashing from the woods not far away. We rushed to the scene to discover our missing classmates trimming the limbs from a perfectly sized living tree they had managed to topple with the help of a hand-saw one of them had brought.

"It was crowded between those two trees and would have died eventually," one student explained.

Lodge Owl was upset. "This wasn't our agreement. Did you even pray for it first? Explain what you were going to do? Make the offering and get the tree's consent? No. Harvesting the dead should not require killing the Living."

The student who cut the tree was confused. He pointed at me. "I don't know about all that. Mr. Walker said we needed a strong baby tree 4"-6" wide and 32'-35' long. And here it is. Right? Listen, man, I'm sorry if I offended you," he said to Lodge Owl. "I'm from Iran. I just came to your country a few months ago. I don't know anything about your customs or agreements over here. That's why I took this class."

Lodge Owl grew very quiet for a moment, then nodded his head. "I see. A true misunderstanding. So — On behalf of this tree, this still living being, we will make our prayers, apologies and offerings now. And prayers to this one's parents…" He pointed to the two redwoods it had been jammed between. They seemed to be leaning into each other, like an embrace. "We must use this tree now or we waste a life. Let's hope our prayers are accepted."

One of us ran back to the truck and came back with the others; it took all twelve of us to hack off the juicy young branches, and we still struggled to haul it back to the truck. By then we were exhausted and didn't have the collective strength to lift it onto the stack of poles already loaded on the flatbed. We put it down for a minute to catch our breaths and consider the situation.

Ali, the Iranian student, studied the situation. "If a couple of you shorter guys stand at the bottom of the pole to hold the base steady and keep it pressed into the ground, maybe the rest of us could stand the pole up straight and lower it onto the truck. You think that would work Mr. Walker?"

I agreed and we arranged ourselves with the shortest, heaviest among us as anchors while the rest of us lined up from shortest at the bottom to tallest at the top near the tip. At the count of three we lifted it, struggling under it, lifting and pushing it up as we walked toward the base, with our anchors holding the end down as the pole lifted up until it was standing upright at the end of the truck. Suddenly the pole shivered, seemed to buck, slipped out of our hands and flopped onto the top of the load with a crash, denting the hood of the truck when it thumped down on top of it. But the load stayed solid!

We stood there astonished and confused. What the hell just happened?

Suddenly Lodge Owl roared in laughter. "Okay, my brothers. I get it. Watch out! This Tipi is Big Medicine, This is going to be a Coyote Tipi! The trees have spoken and they're laughing too. Watch out for that last pole Mr. Walker — it's still alive. It has a mind of its own."

Several of the students scoffed in disbelief, but Lodge Owl grinned. "You'll see. You'll learn how it's all related. We're on a journey of discovery together here and we'll see if you still think it's funny when this is finished."

I cleared my throat. "It suggests that even the trees have a sense of humor, so let me go out on a limb and say — Thank you, Sacred Trees, and thank you young tree. Welcome to our Native American Literature Class. You will be our womb for us to be born into new understandings. And thank you, fellow classmates, for your hearts and your help in this project. What's done is done, and done in good faith. Too late now to change a thing. This Lodge is going to be a place of learning, so let's get this old truck back to the campus, unload it and call it a day."

We tied down the load, then piled into our cars and I drove the truck with Lodge Owl beside me. On the way back to town we discussed the bark skinning tools we would need to rent from a tool rental place in town. We met back at the Well Road on the edge of the upper campus near Porter Gulch Road and drove the rough dirt road back to Kahn's Pond and Bougainvillea Garden. The Horticulture Department had given us permission to construct the tipi there. After unloading the poles onto four 8' square loading pallets we had lined up off the side of the road, I dropped off the truck outside the warehouse where I was told to leave it, dropped the keys into the dropbox, climbed into my van and drove home exhausted, amazed at all that just happened, and astonished that my one big prayer made at the beginning of the project seemed to holding firm: *"Great Spirit. If anyone is to get hurt in this endeavor, please let it be me, not the students."* A prayer which I repeated often. Because today had scared me. And even though this was College with supposedly mature people, I knew that with that living tipi pole we had a potential Brat on our hands!

For the next five weeks over a dozen male and female students, 18-50 years old, some from different countries, worked their butts off to create their vision. From all over the neighborhood children and their parents, students, other faculty members, walked down the Well Road to watch us work, offer advice, even pitch in to help us trim and skin and smooth the trees, then painting them with several gallons of tree oil for preservatives, lavishing them with our prayers and appreciation and laying hands on them every day, turning them from dead trees into tipi poles. It sometimes felt to me like washing the bodies of the dead, while joyously bringing them back to a semblance of life. Eighteen trees were a shiny brown color, but the youngster looked slick and shiny, slightly yellow, and glowed with an attitude all its own. When we finished we were ten weeks into the semesters and it was time to put these poles to use!

Meanwhile our classes were well attended, with at least 30 or 40 members coming each week. We closed the heavy curtains, cutting us off from the cafeteria. The food service officially closed at 7PM. By eight the place was usually empty and the janitors got to work. Often before class small groups would meet discuss their projects and give us reports on their progress. The Associated students had awarded Friends of the Tipi $350 — half the cost of the Tipi Cover. I talked our Department Chair out of another $100 by reminding him how much good will the class was earning the Department by adding all those extras students. Like the High schools, Community Colleges were paid per enrollments, so the added revenue helped the school. The class club held a Bake Sale and Blanket dance on campus and raised another $75.

Then Lodge Owl took me to meet Dan Stolpe at his Native Images studio on the edge of town. Dan embraced me like a Brother from Another Mother and offered to donate some of his colorful lithographs and serigraphs of Buffalos, wild life, birds, and many sepia colored prints from the heavy, hand-carved block prints of his iconic friend and companion — Coyote! There were prints of Coyote Embracing his Lover, Coyote Farting at the Moon, Eating the Moon, Meeting Butterfly, Coyote as Chief, and many more. Amazing work!

At Dan's insistence I selected over a dozen `17' X 26" Prints to show on Campus in a silent Auction to be held in the Cafeteria over a week's time. The Art Department kindly loaned us the easels, but the Janitors were upset with us because they had to move the easels every night when they mopped the floors. However, "Sadi", the Iranian Lady who had just been hired as Director of Food Services, told them to back off and help us to achieve our goals. She believed in teamwork. What a cheerleader she was!

We made the rest of the money from the auction just In time. I drove down to Western Union on Pacific Avenue and wired $750 to Goodwin & Cole, who delivered our finished Tipi cover via UPS to the campus Warehouse where the warehouse workers helped me load the neatly wrapped Eighty pound bundle into my VW bus. I drove up to the cafeteria, parking in back near the produce delivery loading door. I called for three volunteers to help and we hauled the bundle to the middle of the cafeteria floor and unwrapped it. Other students moved the tables and chair to the sides, much to the horror of the night janitor who had just finished sweeping the floor. He calmed down when I promised that we'd put everything back right where he wanted when we were done.

As the students assembled for class they formed a ring around the circle of the tipi with the smoke hole flaps and ties properly folded back on the canvas. The open door seemed to be inviting us in. Lodge Owl entered the room last, accompanied by a tall, smiling dark haired woman in her early fifties. She wore a long, hand stitched blue velvet ceremonial dress, with an abalone shell necklace and matching ear-rings, She also carried a braid of sage in one hand and an Eagle Feather Fan in the other.

Lodge Owl introduced her as Mary Rio Tutar from the Watsonville Amah Mutson Indian Council. She had come to Bless our Tipi and offer prayers at Lodge Owl's request. She carefully unwrapped the bundle he carried, revealing a caved red pipe-stone bowl attached to a foot long wooden stem. A single long feather from the tail of a red Hawk was tied to the stem near the bowl.

"I gathered the *Kinikinik* you asked for," I said, offering

Lodge Owl my pouch. "I followed your recipe. Some of this stuff is hard to find!"

He opened the pouch, smelled it, shook some into his hand and tasted it, rubbed the rest with his figures, then passed the pouch to Mary, who tested it the same way and nodded her approval. Lodge Owl filled the bowl from my pouch and quietly held the pipe high above his head for our attention and waited as the room grew so quiet we could hear the buzz of fluorescents overhead.

"In a dream I was given a vision to put on our Tipi. I give it to you now: All around the bottom paint stick figures holding hands, each of their round heads painted a different color, red, black, white, and yellow, alternating like that all the way around our Lodge. Paint an Elk for Protection on the left side of the door above the People. On the right an Eagle hovers above them, keeping Watch. Near the top of the smoke flaps, paint a comet with its trail curling around once to end behind the deer. The comet is a sign of welcome to the mysterious visitors who will come to us and share their light and disappear again into the Great Mystery. Just like us!"

"Ho!" Shouted several students in agreement. Lodge Owl continued, "First Mary and Mr. Walker will smoke from the pipe. We will *not* pass it around. This pipe was carved from red stone in a quarry only Natives People can access, and it was a gift to me from a Lakota Brother after a sweat. After Mary gives the blessing she will carry burning sage around the circle. If you would like Mary to smudge you with blessings, step forward when we come to you. If you are allergic to smoke, please step back and wave us away. We understand."

I lit a wooden match and held it to the Pipe-stone bowl as Mary took four small sips from the stem, blowing smoke in the four directions. I did the same and passed the pipe to. Lodge Owl, urging him to smoke with us. He Accepted. Then

Mary held the pipe to her heart and spoke a blessing in an ancient language we had never heard. She addressed the Four Directions again, naming each for its power and asking for our protection. Finally she turned to the class and said, "This is good. You have a new home. You have a vision to guide you. You have worked hard to create this and there is no end to what you may learn. My name is Mary Rio Tutar and I'm from Rocky Boy Reservation, where I was raised before moving to Watsonville. On Behalf of the TENA Council, I invite you all to attend our First Red Road Pow-Wow at Indian Camp outside of Hollister next Spring so you can hear our singing and see our dancers in their costumes and feel the power of the drums! If you wish, we will do a fuller ceremony when you put up the Lodge. Thank you for letting me pray with you tonight. Now for the smudging…."

I turned to light the sage bundle when, outside the cafeteria, someone shouted, *"Keep your hands off me!"* followed by the serious sounds of a struggle as the doors burst open. We turned to look and our circle broke as two campus policemen marched right across the tipi cover holding one of my students in a hammerlock between them. "Tell these idiots to let go of me, Mr. Walker! They don't know what the hell they're doing!"

"Wait! Stop! What's happening here?" I demanded. "Release my student and explain yourselves. You're interrupting a class in progress."

"That doesn't matter," one cop said. "We're here on a complaint and this one was smoking a joint outside the cafeteria!"

"It's NOT POT you asshole! I told you! It's an Indian *Bidi cigarette*? Don't they teach you anything in your police classes?"

"Who's the teacher here?" The cop demanded, looking into my eyes.

"I am, you know it, and at this moment I'm your teacher too. You have just violated a school prohibition about disrupting classes."

"What class?" he looked around smugly." Someone called our office and reported that a group of people were in the Cafeteria, which is supposed to be closed, smoking pot in a pipe. Is that the pipe?" He pointed at the pipe in Lodge Owl's hands. "We'll need to take it in for testing. Where did you get the pot?"

"There is no pot in that pipe," I said firmly. "That pipe is a sacred object and you will not touch or profane it. As for what's in it, I mixed the *Kinikinik* myself, and can vouch for every ingredient." I showed him my pouch and he took it from my hand and smelled it.

"Good. This is all the evidence we need. I'm taking this back to our lab for testing."

At this point, nearly every one in the class spontaneously, shouted "NO!" so loud the cop dropped the pouch and jumped back like he had been slapped. I picked up the pouch and turned to the class. "Why do you say No? You know there isn't any pot in here, right?"

"There isn't any in there *now,*" One of my students affirmed. "But that doesn't mean there won't be some in there tomorrow morning."

Both cops blushed bright red with shame because they and I knew the students were right, They *might* think of planting some pot to cover their asses.

"Okay," I said to the student cop. "I know you guys are aware that I'm an ex San Francisco Policeman, and I do know about Proper Procedures. I'm not stupid, and you guys are way out of line. Who called this in?"

"We're not at liberty to say," he said.

I glanced around the cafeteria and saw the night janitor

grinning back by the exit door. "Okay, Here's what we're going to do," I said to the cop. "I know you have a locked evidence box back at your headquarters. Four of my students are going to walk back there with you. They, not you, will carry the medicine pouch. They, not you, will place it in the evidence box and watch you seal it. And I'm going to write up a report tonight to describe this incident in detail, including your disrespectful behavior. Note that we have at least 40 credible witnesses to back me up. Right now I have a class to teach, we have work to do and you are standing on our new Tipi cover with your dirty shoes." They looked down at the floor, surprised. "Okay, who wants to walk the evidence back to the campus police office?"

"Me! Count me in! Over here!" Many voices responded.

"I want my *Bidi* butt to go into that box along with the pouch so they don't try and frame me too!" *Bidi* boy demanded. "I have the package wrapper to put in with it."

In less than a minute Bidi Boys and three women walked the policemen through the cafeteria door past the grinning janitor, leading the officers back to their Station.

To diffuse some of the tension, I gave the class a ten minute break. Lodge Owl left with Mary and returned when we reconvened to paint Lodge Owl's vision onto the canvas. Although the class officially ended at 9:30PM, at least a dozen of us stayed late to finish the job. It was fast drying paint, so by 10:30PM we were able to carefully fold the canvas back into a package we could carry out to my bus and store in the Warehouse until we could mount it later in an opening ceremony. The nice part was that the janitor also had to stay late, due to all the delays. But I didn't confront him. I wasn't even all that mad at him, because from his perspective I could understand his misinterpretation of events, especially since he clearly didn't like hippies, and liked Indians even less. I could be snide with him or mean, but he was just a working stiff like me, doing his best as he saw it, and I had to keep working with him for the rest of our duration at Cabrillo, Compared to the Police Officers I had worked with in San Francisco, he was practically a Liberal. I smiled and waved to him as I left, saying, "Sorry to keep you here this long. I'll recommend to Billy Paul that you get paid overtime for all your help!"

After considering the event from many viewpoints, I wrote a carefully worded incident report when I got home, detailing actions, arguments, and conclusions. The next morning when I handed it to Gene Wright, Dean in charge of the Campus Police, he smiled guiltily. "I heard there was a little excitement last night, especially for an English Class."

"So where are the handcuffs?" I asked, holding out my wrists.

"You're good, Walker. No pot was found," Gene said.

"And the *Bidi*?"

"It was just a *Bidi*, of course. They *do* smell weird, you can't blame the cop."

"I don't blame *him*, but it's a shame that he didn't even recognize the smell of real pot, or none of this would have happened. Back at the Academy in San Francisco they at least brought out a kilo of commercial pot so we could see, touch, and smell it fresh. They even fired some up so we could smell it burning, too. You never forget that kind of experience. It makes for better policing."

"They won't let us do that here," Gene sighed. "In so many ways our hands are tied by the system."

"Not tied — Cuffed!" We both laughed.

"Seriously, Walker, I'm worried this tipi thing is going to be a problem for us."

"It already is," I admitted. "But that's exactly what makes it a great educational opportunity as well. Either way, we're going to learn from it, which is what we're here for, right? And when we're learning new things we're bound to make a few mistakes. That's where tolerance and understanding come in — not qualities I claim for myself, but I'm working on them. And just so you know in advance, we'll be putting the tipi up next week about two hours before class down near Khan's pond. We're going to have another ceremony with the same pipe and *kinikinik*, so I need my pouch back. We have some visiting dignitaries from our local Watsonville tribe coming as well. If you do send any officers, be sure they stay back out of the way of the actual class itself, as it states clearly in the Cabrillo Code. Of course, we always welcome Police help in an emergency." We shook hands and I went back to my office to phone *Bidi* Boy and tell him he was off the hook.

3.

Three weeks before the end of the semester we lifted our Class Dream-Vision into the world of Learning. Hours earlier I had arrived at the Well Road staging area to meet with the students who had worked to prepare the poles. Now we had to assemble them. We looked over the stack and chose the three thickest poles to form the triad base. As we carried them to the thirty foot circle we had cleared, the young pole rolled off the stack onto the road. Astonished, we laid out the ones we carried and went back for it.

"Look, Mr. Walker — this one is much thicker than the one we have for the anchor. Why not use this one instead?" One of the students asked.

Lodge Owl and I glanced at each other, alarmed. We looked down at the pole and I swear I saw it quiver in response.

Lodge Owl shrugged. "If that's what it wants…"

"But will it cooperate?" I wondered.

We were all quiet for a moment, contemplating the tree.

Suddenly a sweet minty smell came to us on a breeze and Lodge Owl smiled. "Yes," he affirmed.

All twelve of us carried it to the clearing and exchanged it for the other anchor pole, which we decided to use for one of the door poles. I carefully looped the guide rope around all three at their thinning tips to hold the poles when we lifted them, two together and the third at 90 degree angle.

When we were ready I called "Ho!" and we lifted them slowly into the air by walking them up, then moving the third pole to the East where it would become the other half of our door poles. I walked around the structure, tugging the guide rope tight to secure the tripod. I purposely patted the young tree and thanked it for cooperating, then guided the notching of 15 more poles, five per side, starting with the "extra" stout pole to hold the other side of the open door, then finished by walking around the structure four times, pulling the rope tighter with each turn and then staking it.

The outer skin was attached to the last pole, and we carefully opened it and spread it out around the skeleton so they overlapped by the door, stitching it together with 12 one-foot long wooden "pins" that we pushed through the opposing grouted pin holes.

As we finished attaching the door flap and preparing the interior, a station wagon pulled into the small parking area near the storage sheds and four figures emerged. Mary Rio Tutar from the Indian Council wore a beautiful robe with a colorful bird feather collar, her jet black hair streaked with gray. Next to her was the artist Daniel Stolpe and Lodge Owl, followed bye a large long haired man wearing a black Stetson hat with a large Red Tailed Hawk feather fixed to the brim. He wore a long brown leather coat and carried a guitar case.

Stolpe pointed to me and the stranger walked over. "Floyd Weston, Lakota Sioux recording artist at your service." He

winked, stepped back, looked long at the tipi and laughed.
"Well now, ain't that something? A genuine Tipi on a College
campus? They're going to love hearing this back on the Res."

Mary walked over to the tipi, examining the painted figures
holding hands, exclaiming over the drawings of Elk and Eagle,
then pointed at the comet, laughing. "This is what you hippies
would call 'far out'! Let's see the rest…"

She bowed her head as she stepped inside. We all did. One
after another, everyone had to bow and lower themselves to
enter this high place. We had dug a shallow depression in the
center and lined it with nearby river stones and gravel. A small
careful pile of wood was stacked in the center. To the left of
the door were two five gallon buckets, one of water, the outer
sand. I also brought a Fire Extinguisher from home.

"You will need an inner liner to go all around up to at least
here," Mary said, measuring the height of four feet with her
hand. "Tie it to the poles and It will hold in the heat and keep
out the drafts. But otherwise this is good!" She walked around
the fire pit, looking up through the smoke hole where all the
poles crossed. She stopped at the anchor pole, touched it with
both hands and looked up, surprised. "This one is awake," she
said, surprised.

"Don't worry, it won't bite," Floyd assured her. He winked
at me. I'll be damned if this isn't one of the biggest Lodges I've
been in, and I've been in and out of them all of my life!"

Floyd sat down in the Chief's Spot opposite from the door
and took out his guitar. I dropped my leather shoulder bag
beside him and sank down gratefully. It had been a long day.
Mary and Stolpe sat to Floyd's right. "After our AA meeting
this afternoon, Danny Boy here suggested we come by and
check this place out. Since me being a genuine *Injun* and all,
who is only going to be in town one more day on my way
to LA for a recording gig with Buffy St. Marie, I said, sure,

why not?" He tuned his guitar, bending notes as he talked. "I wish they'd put-up one of those recording studios in Boise or someplace central, kind of mid-way. If they want to record *Injuns*, they should go where we are!"

Students were coming in while Floyd talked. Many students had been walking around the tipi, checking out the paintings, proudly pointing out the parts they had painted. It took a little longer than usual before we were all quietly assembled in a circle for our first class 'in- house', so to speak. It was mid-November and night came quickly to this gully between hills; rain was coming soon. Yet inside the tipi the light still held, shining through the newly born skin. It felt amazing.

The class settled in and I introduced Floyd and asked him if he would say a few words in blessing. He agreed and started to thump his guitar with what he called a pow-wow rhythm using a single chord. Quietly at first, then gradually gaining volume, Floyd began to sing in Lakota, a wavering cry that sent shivers up our spines and tears sprang from our eyes. We didn't understand a word of what he said, but something essential, non-verbal, got through. The song went on for about five minutes, building tempo until it stopped, suddenly. But our heartbeats still pulsed with that rhythm and the song filled our heads.

"*Ho!*" I said when he finished.

Floyd looked around at us, nodded, and said, "That should hold you for a while. But I advise you to move this to a better spot before the rains come and wash you away. It's your business, of course, but I'd hate to see a good Lodge wasted through ignorance. You do know that the Tipi is Turtle Island's first mobile home, right? Whole tribes would pack up and move, following the Buffalo or getting the hell out of the way of the white man, dragging the poles with horses or by hand to wherever the next site was found. No camping permits needed back then!" He glanced at his watch. "Well, I see it's time for me to be moving on, too. Thank you for inviting me here tonight. Good luck in your new home."

Floyd quickly packed up his guitar, then he, Mary and Stolpe got up together, shook my hand, shook Lodge Owl's hand, waved to the class and quietly slipped through the door hole and were gone. We heard the station wagon turn around and drive slowly back down the rutted Road.

Lodge Owl put away his pipe. "No need for this, Mr. Walker. We have been blessed."

"Do you know what he said when he sang?" Someone asked from the circle.

"No. But do you know what the Priest is saying in Catholic Church when he talks on Sunday? Maybe not, but I sure know when I have been blessed," Lodge Owl said.

"I think you're right," I agreed. "And now that we're here, let me remind everyone that your Final Papers are due next week." The class groaned. "I know how you feel, but that only gives me one week to read your papers, record your grades, and return them to you for our last class in two weeks. Remember, you can opt to take the class for credit only, but you need to tell me that by next week,"

I moved to the fire pit, knelt down, lit a wooden match and held it to the duff and dry tinder at the middle of the fire, fanning the small flames larger with a black crow feather I had found near the tipi poles. When I sat back down I waited a few minutes, watching the flames chew on the harder wood. A trance-like atmosphere fell over us as we watched the flames. I realized that people have been doing this for a million years!

"We are now in Native American Space, Indigenous space, Round Space. We have circled back in time, and Winter is the time for Stories! So tonight let's discuss some of the stories we've heard, the texts, the speakers, the tipi, the whole semester! How did any of this work for you? What did you learn? I'd ask if you got your money's worth, but Cabrillo doesn't charge tuition, so all of this was free except for the valuable time you invested in the readings and all your work creating our collective dream. What stories did you like most? Which speakers? Who wants to go first?"

Many hands waved, so we talked clockwise around the circle, many voices asking, responding, arguing, laughing, and by the time we had done this a few times class was over. As I left that evening, after making sure the fire was out, I bowed my head to the spirit of the tipi and stepped back into Anglo Time, attaching the door cover. I left some wood and the buckets, but took the fire extinguisher with me when I left.

Our timing remained impeccable through the end of the semester. The morning after our last class we took down the tipi, laying the poles back on their resting rack of pallets.

We rolled up the tipi's skin and stored it in the Warehouse until Spring, That afternoon it started to rain, and continued storming until the end of March.

4.

Spring semester was well under way and my second batch of English 24 students were clamoring to put up the tipi. This was a whole new crop of students, tipi virgins ignorant of the dangers, thirsty for the rewards of lived experience. I shared some of what I had learned last semester, and reminded them that it wasn't my tipi, it belonged to the associated Students of Cabrillo College, and if they wanted it put back up they would have to do it themselves. To my surprise, over 3/4 of the volunteers to do the work were women this time around, a complete flip of the original group. But they were strong, determined ladies from 18 to 50 years old and ready to rip, so I agreed.

The Well Road was still muddy from the rains, and the flooded area where we set up originally would not work now. Lodge Owl wasn't in this semester's class, having transferred to UCSC, but he showed up and walked the campus with me to Identify possible spots. Best of all was where we held our first meeting, but the top of the hill was too public for our purpose. However, a flat area further back down on the side of the hill next to the old wooden water tower looked perfect. We could easily bring the poles up the semi-paved access road, and run a hose from the water tower to the tipi so we had access to running water in case of fire.

After some discussion, I got the okay from Floyd Younger, our Dean of Instruction, to move the tipi up there. Out of sight out of mind was best, in his opinion. He said he was already getting complaints from some in the community and we only had it up for three weeks last semester. I assured him no-one was camping in it.

Once again we borrowed Cabrillo's flatbed truck to haul the polls down the well road, make a wicked U-turn, then drive them up the access road nearly half a mile to the water tower above the campus, where we unloaded them close to the road. It took two trips to make it easier, and I returned the truck muddy but undamaged this time. Curiously, no-one ever said a word about the dented hood.

We had just finished lifting the lodge, and I was winding the 50 foot long 3/8" rope around the poles, when I heard a vehicle stop on the road. A few minutes later Dan, Mary, and Lodge Own came around the water tower, followed slowly by a large long-haired man with a face chiseled out of stone. Like Floyd he wore a large cowboy hat, this one White sprouting four Eagle wing feathers. Like Floyd, he wore a heavy leather jacket, worn blue jeans and black cowboy boots. I wondered if the two were related.

They all paused, staring at the tipi with appreciation, Suddenly the big guy broke into laughter. "Ha! You weren't shitting me after all, Dan. This thing really is bigger than the ones we have at DQ University. How the hell did they pull this off?" He came over to where Dan was shaking my hand.

His grip was strong and he looked straight into my soul. "I'm Dennis Banks, President of DQ University. You the teacher here?"

"More like a facilitator. I'm just learning about Native People like the rest of the class."

"Well that's one place to start," he agreed. "Who's vision's on the skin?"

"That was Lodge Owl's dream, but everyone helped paint it. Walk around and check it out. Check inside, too. You're welcome here. You guys invented it, after all — Turtle Island's first Mobile Home?"

"An old joke on the Rez, but true. Let's see what you got here." Dennis walked around the tipi, them joined Mary and the rest of us inside.

By now the class was trickling in, and we all stood for the opening ceremony. At my invitation, Dennis produced a pipe, pre-packed with his own mix — mostly tobacco — He spoke a prayer for the safety of the tipi and all within it in his wonderful 10,000 year old Lakota Language. Then Mary carried around burning sage and fanned blessings on all who invited her — starting with Dennis, who seemed to bathe in the heavy smoke, rubbing it over his head and body. After the Blessing, we sat down and he spoke to us briefly about his mission to walk across America from Wounded Knee to the Department of the Interior in Washington to present their Nation's many grievances and demands to the bureaucrats in person. He had just come from UCSC to speak to students there and raise funds for the walk. He said dozens would start and thousands would finish the walk, a kind of reverse of the original march of *The Trail of Tears* when over 100,000 Indians were forced at gunpoint to march two thousand miles from their homes in the Southeast to the barren lands of Oklahoma.

Lodge Owl asked for Dennis's hat, put in some money, and passed the hat around the circle while Dennis talked. Many of us put in Money for his journey, and by the time it got back to Lodge Owl there was way over $100 and change inside. After speaking about ten minutes Dennis looked around the tipi and nodded at Dan… "What do you say we let these folks get on with their business?"

Dan nodded. All four of them stood up and Dennis took a last look around. "Yes. This is Good. Now listen, if any of you get up to Sacramento, drop by DQ University, the only all Indian University in the country. I am currently the President of the College, but we are so underfunded we hardly exist. About 199 of us live on a corner of the abandoned Mather Air Force Base and use the old barracks and cafeteria for our buildings. We also have two Tipis, a Pomo style stick house, and a Sweat Lodge for invitation only ceremonies. We host a Red Road Pow Wow every year, and Mary's group wants to hold one down at Indian camp sometime this summer."

He turned to Dan. "Ready, Roadies? Let's Rock and Roll! *Ho, Mataquiase!*" One by one they followed Dennis out of the Lodge.

After that we got down to business, discussing texts and papers due and I reminded the class that we worked on two schedules in this class — one was academic, with dates for tests and grades; the other was unwritten, because guests speakers were going to show up often and I had no idea who or when because they ran on Indian time, which was more flexible. We were going to do both, to the best of our abilities.

At least that was our intent.

5.

Up to this point I have provided the context for the Coyote Tipi. Now I will present some of the delicious content, brought by the story tellers themselves as food for our hungry hearts. Because there were so many speakers and notes over time, I had to be selective. I have tried to be true to their words, which we often wrote by firelight in our notebooks. I take responsibility for any errors which may appear.

Joseph Lumi, Medicine Man from the State of Washington. "Sometimes people ask me how old I am and they are surprised when I confess I don't know. When I was a small child I was taken from my parents and sent to a far away school in Canada where the nuns burned our tongues with candle flames when they caught us talking our Native Language. But I do remember my Initiation into the tribe just a while before the Whites snatched me away. I remember one morning Grandfather woke me up early. It was still dark out. "Come with me, grandson, it's time to meet our Guardians." He took me by the hand and we walked through our little village to his boat. Grandpa helped me inside where I sat right in the middle while he rowed far out on the Bay of Puget Sound, where we stopped and waited. Then Grandpa started singing a little song, over and over." Joseph hummed the song for a few seconds to show he remembered. "Then, all of a sudden the water heaved up and the boat rocked and there besides us was a huge whale, and his big eye was staring right at me. "Good morning, Brother," Grandpa said to the whale. "It's time to meet your grandson." Then he picked me up and placed me right up there on top of that whale's back. And you know what? That whale spouted water and it poured down on us like rain and we laughed and I held up my hands and felt so happy! We sat like that for a long time, but it was too short a time, and I was sad when Grandpa picked me up and plopped me back in the boat. Then, without a sound, the whale sank into the water and disappeared and Grandpa rowed us back home. I remember a few other things about those days, too... how Indian children were born next to a river or creek, how ceremonies still made the crops grow, how all the treaties were illegal, how my people never ceded the salmon or the buffalo or the trees — even the minerals were dug up and everything slaughtered and taken away!"

Oh-Shinnah, Canadian Cherokee: "I lived my early years in the Four Corners area. That is the area in the Southwest where Colorado, New Mexico, Utah, and Arizona conjunct in a cross. Where I come from the Indian People call that place 'The Heart of the Mother'. As our hearts have magnetic field, so does our Mother Earth. Greed is about to rip open the Heart of our Mother. Greed for energy and resources they have no right to! It seems insane to me that the Hopi People are not being heard. They are an Elder race — a link to our ancient past. Not only will Hopi be destroyed, but our Mother's Heart as well. Do you know what that means? Do you understand magnetic energy? I feel pain right here in my heart. I don't understand why we, as conscious, supposedly intelligent human beings, allow it to continue. And we do allow it. Every time we turn on the electricity we allow it. Every time we get in a car, we allow it. Did you know that all the energy in one crystal can generate enough electricity to run this whole school? The ancients had crystals for healing and for communication, for all sorts of things. The Old Way is still here — the Esoteric is not going to be esoteric very much longer. One of things my father told me was that This is the age. There will come a time in your life when the mysteries of all the Peoples of the earth will be revealed to each other.

Oh Children of the Dawn, Awake! To become a human being is something we must actively pursue in consciousness. A lot of consciousness is developing in various movements and new religious and I think they are all good. I think the influx of the eastern way into the west is good, but it is not all. Few of these traditions do anything about the responsibility they may feel for Earth Mother. Now more and more Indian people are coming out and talking to people like you, as an outgrowth of that responsibility. We were given the sacred duty to take care of the Earth Mother, and we are not being allowed to fulfill our function. People are not listening to us.

"Look at the weather changes! Imbalances are being inflicted upon Nature, and Nature is speaking out against that imbalance. It is trying to correct itself but it can't — we keep ripping it apart! It's your Earth, it's your water, those are your trees — not in a sense of ownership, but in a sense of Oneness. I really feel physical pain in my heart when I see what has happened to my planet, to my Mother. She gives us everything we have, she feeds us, she clothes us. I don't believe that there is any health for anybody until something is done about the environment. What you call Ecology I call Religion. Somebody asked me once, 'What is the Indian Religion?' Ask each individual Indian and you will get a different story from any one of them because it is really an individual thing. But it is all based on relationship with the Earth Mother and the responsibility that one has to the Earth. And all that healing that you are doing on yourself doesn't mean anything if you let your Mother die! We need to take care of our own Garbage..

"I know that Teachers are important, that we need them in our lives. But we are not supposed to follow in their footsteps. We need to make footsteps of our own. Instead we are becoming shadows. I believe that we are supposed to be

individuals and it is through the individualization of self that
we reach Conscious Perfect Being. This vision I share is a
moment of illumination, a moment of cosmic consciousness.
It is *Being At One with The One.* Coming back from that place,
it's different. You have to take your visions and implement
them into reality. The only way we're going to have a world
community where the children are free is if we free ourselves.
You have to be willing to stand up for what you believe. If you
don't, then you are just talking. There are children starving to
death here in this country right now — Indian children, black
children, white children — for a fact! Immigrants everywhere.
The children are hungry and we throw grain into the ocean.

We're crazy. We are a psychotic people. We live in a
psychotic society and what's more, we are complacent. I
get that way myself. If you see somebody being harassed
in the street and you don't do something about it, you are
contributing to it.

"Who are your brothers and sisters? What form does your
prejudice take? On the other side of the earth that sacred
trust is held by the People of Tibet. They hold the balance
of the Earth in their ceremonial lives, in their Spiritual lives.
On this side of the Earth are the Hopis. The Tibetan is the
masculine energy; over here it is the feminine energy. A lot of
the Tibetans have come to the United States, to Canada, and
to Peru. All that energy is coming over to this continent right
now to help. Not too long ago we brought together a meeting
of my grandfather David of Hopi, and one of the Tibetans,
Gorman Rinpoche, who is affiliated with No Hung Rinpoche,
Keeper of Tibetan Prophecy. One of the things they found out
was that the Hopi word for Moon is the Tibetan word for Sun,
and the Hopi word for Sun is the Tibetan word for Moon, The
similarities in Spirituality are just incredible, except that one is
more masculine and one is feminine. "What is the difference

between male and female, masculine and feminine? Besides the obvious biological differences, it is a matter of spirit. Women are the Givers of Life. It is through our own body processes that Life comes forth, and because of that we have an intuitive nature. I think you have to be more open to give life to bring forth children. You have to understand the basics about what Life is all about.

"It's important in this day and age that we stand up for what we believe in, What do we believe? I believe that if you are sick, you can heal yourself. I know that is possible to do anything that you decide to do, and I am going to tell you how that works. Everything that exists was brought about into material because of a man or a woman's ability to conceive. That which you can conceive of you can bring about into your material reality If you can think of it, see it before you, keep that image in front of you at all times, you will get what you want. I know it is true from experience.

"One of the things my Elders told me was that wherever I went, no matter what I did, I should leave that situation better than it was when I got there. That means the physical environment as well as people. It is not enough to just talk about it, you have got to actively involve yourself in what is going on with your environment. No one has authority over your life. If you give them authority over your life, you are subjecting yourself to lesser consciousness. That's why I'm here before you now, to tell you to be Brave. This is your time. Our time. Thank you for letting me speak."

Abalone, an activist trying to stop the building of a nuclear plant near Santa Barbara, came to the tipi with two women from Big Mountain. He delivered this message, sent to all Earth People by **David Kartchongva, Hopi Sun Clan Leader, Big Mountain:**

"I AM THE SUN, the Father! With my warmth all things are created. You are my children, and I am very concerned about you. I hold you to protect you from harm, but my heart is sad to see you leaving my protecting arms and destroying yourselves. From the breast of your mother, the Earth you receive your nourishment, but she is too dangerously ill to give you pure food. What will it be? Will you lift your Father's heart? Will you cure your mother's ills? Or will you forsake us and leave us with sadness, to be withered away? I don't want this world to be destroyed. If this world is saved you will all be saved, and whoever has stood fast will complete the plan with us, so that we will all be happy in the Peaceful Way. People everywhere must give Hopi their most serious consideration, our prophecies, our teachings, and our ceremonial duties, for if Hopi fails, it will trigger the destruction of the world and all mankind. Blood will flow and our clothing will be scattered on the earth. Nature will speak to us with its mighty breath of wind. There will be earthquakes and floods, causing great disasters, changes in the seasons and in the weather, disappearance of wildlife, and famine in different forms. There will be gradual corruption and confusion among the leaders and the people all over the world, and wars will come about like powerful winds. All of this has been planned from the beginning of creation. I have spoken through the mouth of the Creator. May the Great Spirit guide you on the right path."

Roberta Blackfoot and **Paulee Whitesinger** from Big Mountain came with Abalone to discuss their protest against Peabody Cole and urge students to join them on Big Mountain during their summer break. They had spoken at UCS the night before. With trembling voices, these small but fierce grandmothers stood up for their lives.

Roberta Blackfoot: "I'm not going to sign up for relocation from my native land! I will stay there. They can do anything they want with me but I will not move. My goats will not leave me. Maybe I'm getting tired. That's all I have to say."

Roberta sat down. **Paulee** continued," I'm Dineh, born on Big Mountain 57 years ago. I live there with my ancestors. US Government says I don't belong there. I never been to school, don't believe in Public Law, All my life I have kept the peace, carried the bundle, made offerings to the Mountain where we get our spiritual strength. This whole thing makes me angry, disturbs our peace, scatters our prayers. Don't you know that to relocate means to move away and never be seen again?

Now you have helicopters and Phantom Jets buzzing over our reservation to drive us away. But we're not leaving! We are Big Mountain!

Wallace Black Elk and Grace Spotted Eagle — (WBE's 1/2 Self) Lakota Sioux: "*Ho, Mataquiaes!* means 'All my Relations,' in my language, Lakota, which is thousands of years old. I have come to speak to you tonight because you couldn't come to me out on that reservation. Reservations are little concentration camps created by the US Government to lock up people who were free. When the white man came, he saw that Tipi's door is always open, so he walked in and stole everything — our homes, our land, our culture, our religion, our pride. What about all those commandments the Jesus People use as a shield to hide behind?: 'Love thy neighbor, Thou shall not lie, thou shall not kill, thou shall not steal…?' They creep up close with sweet words and then they grab you. They say follow these rules or else, but they don't do it themselves.

'I can see right off that some of you are getting uncomfortable, but that's all right. If I can survive you for the past five hundred years, you can survive me for one night. You

never heard what I think because you never asked until now.
When your teacher asked us to speak he wanted to know what
we were going to tell you. I said, I have no idea. Well, when
can you come? I have no idea, I told him. Earth People don't
have no weekends, no Sundays or Fridays, no September or
May. For us, every day is now, and it has a beginning and an
end. So that's why we came tonight, because he asked us, even
though we're not on your schedule.

"Just to set the record straight, I'm not an Indian. I'm
not an American, either. I'm an Earthman, a living book,
and I'm proof that John Wayne didn't kill us all off or all
die of diseases. In spite of the history books, we're still here.
Remember that the victors wrote those histories, but they
don't always tell the truth. The truth is embarrassing. The
Truth is genocide.

"Back in BC — Before Columbus — there were over 250
Earth People languages, one for every nation. There are many
other languages as well — the Eagles, Buffalo, Deer, Bears,
Butterflies, even little ants, they all have their own brains,
hearts, spirits, and languages. Mother Earth speaks with many
voices. Even the plants are talking to each other, but we can't
hear them anymore. Back in BC we could all speak to each
other. Now it's all static and noise and beer commercials on
the radio and TV. It's the same city at the end of every road,
filled with the same Denny's or McDonald's, the roaring of
trucks and buses and cars. Now we can't hear anything, not
even ourselves. We forgot how to listen.

'What if I was to tell you that a prophecy from nine
generations ago said a society would be here and create a
monster which would grow real fast and try to swallow the
world. But there's fire in the rock which he'll explode and
blow his head off. Would you listen to it? It's a modern story,
I think. This Apocalypse! It already happened to us Indians.

So who is this Government that is out of control? Who is responsible? This guy Ronnie What's-his-name bought and paid for all these bombs and things with your money. He believes in Armageddon, and if he wants to use them who's going to stop him? I hear he's even making war on the Stars.

"And that brings us up to date, From BC to AD. To us ignorant Indians AD means Atomic Destruction. But what do we know? We're just savages."

Grace Spotted Eagle, WBE's 1/2 Self: "We were planted here by the Great Spirit, everything living together in harmony. Our ancestors didn't need no refrigerators or electricity. They dried their meat and berries. They knew the arts of survival. I want to say that in our tradition there is no such thing as a Medicine Man or Woman. We are only spiritual consultants, guided by spirits. Grandmother Earth is the only medicine woman, and what your grandma teaches you is free. She grows all the medicine and herbs, she alone knows what is good for us. All that uranium, coal, and oil inside her keeps us in balance. When you rip minerals out of her, she gets sick. She grew you, just like she grew all the four-legged, the winged, the insects and fish. We are all related, and whatever you do to your mother you do to yourself. So if Mother Earth is injured, where is she going to go for help? She has to shake it off, to purify herself. That's all those earthquakes and floods. Scientists who pollute say, 'We're just doing our job, but the effects aren't our problem.' Whether they cure you or kill you, it costs like hell and then they charge you to bury you.

"All my life I was taught to keep back, to shut up, to stay in the kitchen and cook. Then one day in 1973 at Wounded Knee a newsman put a microphone in front of my face and asked me to say something.. So I did, and I've been talking ever since. I don't talk that Washington D.C. language or that college talk, either. But our Grandmothers were the back bones of our Grandfathers; it's time women put in their two cents about how this country should be run. I want to say right off that women are not 'ribs', no matter what it says in the Bible. God didn't take a crooked rib and create a crooked woman for Adam, and it's not all her fault we're in this mess today. It's not true either that only man has a soul, not women or animals. These ideas divide us. We have all been brainwashed."

Wallace Black Elk: I'm trying like hell to understand the American Way of Life. Constitution says, 'We the People, but are Indians People? Some people say we should stay in our concentration camp reservations where we are kept helpless, not go around talking to you. They say we're ignorant savages who only think of shooting deer. But look at your CIA and FBI and Police — who are they shooting at? Put a picture of your children or someone you love up next to their targets and you'll know. We make a prayer and maybe kill a deer to eat for food and clothing. But your giant Nationals demand everything at gunpoint and we are all prisoners and hostages to them. The Buffalo were replaced by Safeway and stale cheese. You have four walls, a box, a city, a state; you have a door, but you are not free. You need to lock yourselves inside and keep a loaded shotgun by your door because you let evil power roam your streets.

Grace Spotted Eagle: What does Peace and Goodwill mean for this society? It means prepare for war! An evil spirit is loose in your society, full of lusts and hatred. It gets into people and makes us rape and kill each other. It even makes animals crazy, bears attacking people, things like that. It's time now, in this circle of life, where everything happens twice.

Lincoln and Kennedy, Wounded knee in 1890 and again

in 1973, people wearing beads and long hair again, seeking the old ways. Spirit is rising again, searching for identity. Our future is our past and our past is our future, because everything is a circle, like the seasons that come round again. Purification starts in the mind. Personal purification is possible and can alter things.

"The Sacred Fire is in each of our hearts, just as it is in our Grandmother Earth. That fire is your friend, you can talk to it, and if you listen you can hear it talk to you. If your heart spark goes out you will grow cold and indifferent to others; you won't be able to give hugs or smiles or forgive. Fire and water together are great purifiers. Fire cooks food and heats the stone people for our sweats. Weather changes, earthquakes, floods, these things are Grandmother Earth trying to awaken her children so we can start healing and mending the world. We have grandchildren, and we don't want the world to be destroyed. We know that the world itself won't end, but people might! Grandmother Earth will keep living and bringing forth the generations without us. I was taught as a child that whatever you think is a prayer that will come to pass. So we were taught to be careful what we think and say, especially in anger, because once the words leave your mouth you can never take them back."

Wallace Black Elk: Earth People are here to break through the civilized shell and heal each other and the Earth. We have to stop drinking wine and those six packs of poison and all of those other drugs so we can stop being confused. We need clear minds to see our way and leaders who aren't drinking champagne all the time. We already have enough nerve gas to kill the earth's population ten times over, plus all those tens of thousands of nuclear bombs. The other day I looked around and saw that my people were dying, Alcohol, broken homes, sickness, jails; but not only two leggeds — animals, fish, even the plants and trees are dying around me. I was crying to see everything dying, when Grandmother came with a cane and a crystal, sweet winds and sweet smells. I saw her scattering tiny grains of soil from her hand, and they blew out over the ground on the winds as she said, 'I have Countless Love for my children.' So she sent us, and that's why we're talking to you today. Thank you. *Ho, Mataquiase!*"

Willard Pipe Boy, Sioux, Rosebud Reservation: "Sometimes I'm asked how I feel about non-Indians studying Medicine Ways. It depends on who and how. It is possible. If you can fast and pray sincerely to the Great Spirit, some of the mysteries of the Planet Earth may be shown to you You can be anybody, but if you try hard enough it can be done. One of my Teachers was Bill Schwagman, a German Chief and Medicine Man. He died about four years ago. It was a simple life before the white man came with all his books to confuse everyone. For the Indian people the real school is out there, you walk on it and look at it every day. The food is there — turnips, onions, potatoes, the water, the sun, the animals, they're all there for us. Spring water, the best natural water, is the last there is.

"Indians were accused of worshiping animals, trees, etc., but they pray for all that they are going to live with and sacrifice — every bit of the body gets used in some ways. There is no 'time' when we have to pray, like on Sunday. But to continually give thanks for the things all around us without asking for anything, that's a real prayer. What's out there? The Book of Life is right in front of us. No laws, just guidance.

The Government does make rules regulating religion — it crushed the Indian's! 1929 was the last Sun Dance until we brought it back in the early '50's. Sundance is Sacrifice for the People, it is Humbling ourselves before Maker, four days of fasting, sweats, dancing, and piercing. Only participants are present. If you are there, you are Sundance. I will say no more. They asked me about it down at the Dubuque. Iowa Theological Seminary where they brought me to speak and explain the pipe-ritual. What a Sad Place! Those preachers are very confused people. The Fathers and Nuns were holding a Pow Wow and wanted me to bless it with feathers. They didn't have any Indian Deacons, they can't get jobs in rich areas, they are discriminated against. Bill Blacklance from Rosebud was going to be a Deacon — he's the only one — but he got cancer and Seminary wouldn't pay for his hospital, so he called out to his People and got doctored by a medicine man. He was healed, and he's now in charge of the WICK program at Rosebud. Organized religion stands in the way of experiencing God. Indians worship the Earth and Life, while a white person worships The Book. So Bill gave up his Seminary training for the Indian Ways.

"We follow the path of the pipe. Of course, I couldn't tell them anything about the Pipe because I am a Pipe-Carrier, empowered to lead Sweats, Sundance, Vision Quest and *Yuwipi* ceremonies. These things are sacred, not to be spoken of except in general. *Yuwipi* are guardian angels, medicine men who have died and come back to help the medicine person in trance. They are messengers, spirits, ghosts, the true healers. The medicine man is merely the interpreter. Lots of people want to be medicine men but they don't know what that means. Those who know don't want to be one, more often than not. They have to be called to it by dreams, by inner feelings. You have to go through training to understand the everyday mysteries. I was given a pipe that was 487 years old by Charley White Deer The pipe was broken, but I fixed it and returned it to Charley. That was sweet medicine.

"I don't want you to think that everything I'm going to say is so serious. Sioux have a great sense of humor, but it's often delivered 'deadpan', sometimes right in the middle of ceremonies. There's a little bit of Trickster in each of us. No man is perfect who is walking now — you have to have humor. No matter how honest or perfect, there's always a mistake. In the Beginning of Learning young people go too fast and forget to pray, so sometimes it's sixteen or twenty years before they get it. You could be 38 or 40 years old but only three or four years old in Spirit. You have to learn deep to grow. Our Elders still call us children when we're fifty years old.

"Now one last thing about the Medicine Wheel. There is a huge one in Montana, so big you can only see its whole shape from the air, but our People built it thousands of years ago, and it's still there, still used for prayer. We stand in the center and face the East and the Four Directions come together around the pipe. They enter us through the smoke and prophesies. Spirit will take you and educate you. That is our way. Ho! This is finished."

Over the course of 12 years, dozens of Native People appeared to share their knowledge with my students. Among therm were **Uncle Henry Tyler**, an 86 year old Arapaho Peyote Road Man and Story Teller who would not tell us anything about their Peyote Ceremonies except that Peyote was specifically for healing Indian People, and non-indians should find another way to talk with God. He did tell us that the fire was sacred, and as he whispered to us over the fire, with shadows dancing off the tipi walls, he said that everything was made official over the fire. Once the whites wanted to build two roads that did not cross but ran strong next to each other, one white and one red. The vision was strong and good but it never happened. The meeting was set but the Whitman never came. The Indians waited and waited by the fire, and the fire was witness to the decision. The roads were never built. He whispered several more stories that night but his voice was so low I could not write and listen at the same time. I chose to listen, so the stories will remain in my heart.

Owen Lyons, Iroquois Chief of Six Nations, came to assure us that the Indian's message to us hasn't changed in centuries. The Wild West wasn't "wild" until the white man came. There is no word for 'wild' in any Indian language. The closest you can come is 'free'! Indians aren't 'living' any more, they are into survival. But how are we going to change a system which is corrupted to the roots? No college education is needed to know when Principles are being violated. US laws only serve certain groups. The true regulator is in our own hearts Each of is equal to all things — all life is equal. There is no higher authority. So it takes self-regulation, discipline, to make Principles work. The stronger you are, the more you have to share. All of our gifts are to be shared with each other — not sold. Each of us is born with a mission, something we need to do, and it's up to us to discover what it is. How do we protect these Processes of Survival? We have to inject Spirituality into Government. While Indians were planting Corn, Anglos were planting Flags — what's the first thing they did on the moon? Do they think they own it now?"

6.

After that first year of teaching in the tipi I was ready for a break. I was offered a one year sabbatical, and used it to travel with my wife and 2 & 1/2 year old son to the Middle East, India and Beyond in my quest for Holy Places and Beings.

That adventure must wait until another lifetime to reveal, but while I was gone one of my fellow teachers from the English Department took up the challenge of English 24 and decided to put the Tipi back up in the Fall. Just before we flew away, I warned him about the dangers inherent in treating the tipi casually, like any other classroom. We called it "The Coyote Tipi" for a reason — it was NOT a normal classroom. A tipi is another world — round space, where everything is equal, where knowledge needed to be shared from the heart, not just the head, and none of us were experts and authorities on anything Indian at all. He kept nodding his head, but I wasn't sure he understood.

Stephen was born in England and still had a slight accent even five years after teaching at Cabrillo. He said he was interested in learning about the First Americans. How could I tell him the Tipi did not represent all the different kinds of places real natives lived? This wasn't just a tent to play in The was round space. It wasn't limited by four corners, stale air, and a ceiling pressing us down. The tipi was a living space, filled with lights and shadows and air moving through it carrying the odors of the woods and plants surrounding it, including kids smoking cigarettes outside sometimes. It wasn't always comfortable. It wasn't always safe. No running water or bathrooms nearby. No Janitor to clean it after you leave. You can't play records or show films there. You can't even read from books because the light is dim and at night you need flashlights if you want to reference quotes from any of the books. That's why there was an oral tradition. I tried to discourage him. I felt like I was handing a chain saw to a five year old, but what else could I do? The tipi belonged to the students, not to me. And Steve couldn't put it up alone!

Then I was gone, flying far away on an International journey of discovery and sometimes sheer terror.

Steve, however, followed through with his intention. And his students were thrilled to help him erect the Tipi once again by the water tower. He didn't tell me much about his own experience with the tipi, but at the end of the Fall semester the class published a booklet called *Journal from The Council*

Fire, filled with students writings, poems, photos & drawings created in response to their tipi experience. The Journal was dedicated to Lodge Owl and Mary Rio Tutar (Rocky Boy Reservation — who stepped forward from the class to help Steven with the work). and Linda Kitz for carrying on the tradition of the council fire. Also Thank You to Michael White Elk, whose vision helped make this lodge and this council a reality for us all.

It was a surprise to see that I had been renamed in my absence. But on that night in the cafeteria when Lodge Owl pointed to the tipi and showed us where the Elk should be, he suggested that it not be painted, because the natural coloring of the canvas gave the appearance of real skin. And so it remained, outlined in soft browns and grays.

Alas, in their rush home for Christmas vacation, the class left the tipi up unattended. Around New Year's Eve a ferocious storm blew the tipi down. Three poles were broken, and after the mess was untangled and the cover dried out and stored away, the poles were left where they fell. That Spring class was held back in the classroom,

I returned from my sabbatical about a week before the Fall '75 semester and dropped by the school to check my book orders and reopen my office. When I climbed the water tower road to check on the Tipi, I was shocked to find the Lodge gone and the poles scattered like broken bodies on a battlefield. Steve, bless his heart, had already gone off with his new bride on his own sabbatical year, leaving me to discover the mess on my own. It was Lodge Owl who explained what happened later.

Still reeling from my travels, I wasn't sure what to do. When my Native American Literature students asked me when I was going to put the tipi back up, I admitted exhaustion. I was willing to facilitate, but I could not trim any more trees in this life-time, thank you very much. They would have to do the work themselves. Two thirds of the class were women, from 18 to 60 years old, and after a few minutes discussion I realized that the Women's Movement had manifested on campus, because more then twenty women volunteered to do the work.

And so they did. They also decided to move the tipi to another location, higher up on the hill but a few hundred feet back out of sight from below. When it came time to erect it, Willard Pipe Boy came to town to visit Dan Stolpe and spend a few nights in his studio on his journey south to meet with some Chumash Elders at a Council of Tribes. Mr. Big Oil wanted to put oil rigs off the coast near Santa Barbara and the tribes were alarmed. Their clams, their food, their lives depended on the purity of the ocean, and the waters were already fouled. The Great Ones — the Whales and Dolphin Tribes — were crying for help. They hoped we could stop it by Prayers and Peaceful Protests. Willard said he thought they should use dynamite. Then he burst into laughter to show it was a joke. Or was it? I liked him immediately and asked him if he'd like to bless the tipi. We were putting it up that night at 7pm.

"Is that the tipi you were telling me about, Dan?" Stolpe affirmed. "Hell yes, sounds like a hoot to me." He looked at me suspiciously for a minute, then grinned. "Dan says you guys call it a Coyote, right?" He laughed again. "Don't you know a Coyote is always going to piss on your Tipi and fuck with your woman? It's part of what they do. Dan claims the wind blew it down."

"Yes, during a winter storm. I was half way around the world in India, looking for Holy Men," I said lamely.

"You must be blind then, if you can't see what's in front of you. Why travel all across the world when Holy People are already here? Shaman, Healers, Prophets, Conjourers,

Heyoka's, Yuwipis, Peyote Road Men, Holy Men and Women have been living right here on Turtle Island for thousands of years. But okay, never mind, I see you're still tripping, still searching, so there's hope. You *might* look under your nose! Dan told me you teach in a college, so I don't take it personal. He said you were a seeker, whatever that is. Me, I'm a Finder. I keep finding things I love — a good story, a good meal, great pussy!" He roared with laughter and slapped his thigh. "Sure, let's go take a look at your coyote tipi."

When I arrived at the new site forty or more people were already there, ready to lift the poles and wrap around the skin. I helped coordinate the lifting, placing and tying of the poles. We pinned the flaps and door together with foot long wooden pegs. Two had gone missing in the storm, so our freshly carved redwood pegs gave new color to the door. I stepped inside and placed my fire-hydrant beside a wood pile near the door. The crew had scooped a depression in the center for the fire when we cleared the area.

When I looked up, I was surprised. The new sheen was gone and the skin seemed to be sagging in places because the Re-Erection Group (what one of the ladies in the group called the Tipi Planning Committee) could not find replacements for the broken poles. After a month long failed search for substitutes they decided the do it with three less poles. But it felt like the lodge was missing three ribs. It still felt like a Tipi, but a wounded one. The balance was off. It felt a bit like at the Santa Cruz Mystery Spot out on Branciforte Drive where people seem to shrink or grow in front of your eyes as they walk up or down the hillside and people feel dizzy or nauseous after a very short visit. Yet a million people a year drive out there and pay a few dollars to feel unbalanced. Standing in our Tipi, they could feel unbalanced for free.

The class was seated in a circle and a smudge stick of sage

had passed around when we heard two pairs of boots walking around the tipi and pausing at the door. *"Ho Mataquiase!"*

"Welcome home," I called back. "Tipi door is always Open." Willard Pipe Boy entered first, followed by Dan. I moved aside to give him the Chief's spot and they threaded their way around the circle. Dan sat down cross legged beside me, but Willard Pipe Boy kept standing. He carried a bundle wrapped in red cloth, holding it close as he looked around at the tipi carefully, first at all the people and he grinned to see their smiling upturned faces. So many beautiful Beings. Then he looked around the inside at the tipi itself, pointing at the empty places where the tip skin sagged. He turned around and examined the young anchor pole we called our Coyote Pole. He placed a hand on it, pushing gently, then patted it and frowned, as if listening. He turned to face us.

"This Lodge is a wounded warrior. It is lonely and suffers from neglect. It is three legs short, which you must remedy. It hasn't been staked down, so it can walk away in the night! It also lacks a smoke curtain to run all around the inside to create a draft and carry the smoke upwards. Other wise you will breathe smoke, freeze your butts off in the winter, or burn the place down. But otherwise…? It is big! I don't think I've seen one bigger" He looked closely at the students. "Who's working on this?"

Two dozen hands were raised and he nodded. "You think you can handle those fixes? Every one of them is vital."

"Yes," they agreed.

"Good. Then let's give your home a blessing — since you asked, and since I can see you're going to need another one! You had a good blessing before, but it wore off. Neglect. Abandonment. Listen, now! Tipi is *home*. It wants to be occupied, appreciated, to be Peopled. How can it take care of you, if you don't take care of it? And taking care of each other is everyone's job! That's all I'll say about it." He looked around the circle again, making eye contact with everyone. "Okay? Let's go to work!"

He unwrapped his bundle and paused to display his pipe, holding it up reverently in both hands for all to see. "My name is Willard Pipe Boy, Rosebud Reservation. As you can see, I am a Pipe Carrier and my Job is to help people pray in the Old Way. I'm going to talk to the four directions in my language and then maybe I'll tell you a few things in yours before I go. I'm making tracks for Santa Barbara for a big Pow Wow, and I know your Facilitator here want's to get on with the show. So. This prayer is ten thousand of years old."

He lit the pipe with a red Bic lighter, blew smoke in the four directions, and sang some wavering, mind chilling notes of love and longing. I have no words for the feelings his prayer aroused in us, something different for each of us I'm sure. Then he knelt down, put his pipe away, and spoke to us for another ten or fifteen minutes. While Willard was talking I had slipped $50 to Dan, a kind of standard fee by now that I gave from my own pocket when speakers appeared. When more was required, we did blanket dances, or begged the student council. The College itself had no money for us.

After Willard and Dan left, we fell into a collective silence.

We hadn't lit the sacred fire yet. The rest of the world felt a long way away. It was growing dark outside now and so quiet inside that it felt like we had gone back to the beginning of time. Some of the students were getting nervous.

Then we heard rustling from the bushes behind the anchor pole, something sniffing at the Tipi cover behind me, several other somethings sniffing along the bottom of the Tipi heading toward the door. We grew even quieter and looked expectantly toward the opening. Cautiously, the tip of a black nose sniffed the sage. Then another. And another. One by one a mother deer and her three babies cautiously looked through the door and stared at us, while we stared back, equally astonished. I have no idea how long that moment lasted with all of us quietly gawking at each other, but it felt like a kiss from God.

I blinked and suddenly the deer were gone. The students all turned to look at me. "Class Dismissed," I said. They laughed, but I stood up, stretched, and headed for the door. I left and watched. A few minutes later one or two others left, but I was told later that most of the class stayed until ten and had the best discussion in their lives!

7.

Four days later The Coyote Tipi was stolen from the top of the hill. Not the whole thing. The Tipi had been skinned, slashed from the Poles. The bare skeleton looked violated, with one last smoke flap dangling from the anchor pole. A set of tire tracks circled the frame. The Campus Police Report filed in my mailbox said that the Officers discovered the theft at 6:20AM that morning on a routine patrol to the upper campus. The tire tracks belonged to the campus police car. There was no sign of the Tipi being dragged, and no additional tire tracks — although by the time I arrived over a dozen vehicles had been here, including the County Sheriff and the Capitola Police. But no suspects. No clues. The campus police held the tipi flap for evidence — of what, I'm not sure.

Case dismissed! We laid the Tipi bones back on their pallets and spent the rest of the semester in a classroom, sometimes meeting outside on various lawns and locations for the first half of the class, going in when it grew dark or cold.

The original skin was gone but the bones still had life in them. Turns out that all over the campus, students were

angered by the theft. The women who had worked so hard to
bring it back were outraged at the violation. All their work
and that one magic class had roused their thirst, and they were
determined to put the Tipi up again with a new skin. A small
quiet lady named Kaci from the class said she could sew a
new skin for us on her Industrial Sewing Machine if we could
provide the measurements, material, and physical help to pull
it all together. She had plenty of room in her barn where they
could make it. Almost the entire class volunteered and they
started on the path to Coyote's Reincarnation.

The Cabrillo Administration was not eager to see the Tipi
renewed or put up again on the hill top where it was clearly at
risk, or anywhere else, for that matter. But the student Council
was happy to see the class continued. When the Friends of
the Tipi student club requested help, the Council Voted to
fund the new canvas in full. The Administration was not
happy, but accepted the decision (after reading me the riot
act, listing all the state codes we were potentially violating).
But They insisted when it finally occurred, that we put the
Tipi up on the lower campus meadow behind the old Sesnon
House, an Abandoned mansion that came with the property
when Cabrillo bought it for a campus. The College was already
renewing the building, bringing it up to code so they could
add a Food Services and Cooking Classes to the curriculum.

The Campus Police Building on the lower campus was
barely 100 feet away, but that was far enough to satisfy the
students. Screens of trees hid us and the whole meadow from
view from nearly every direction. There were bathrooms
in the Police building and a hose we could run across the
lawn under the Tipi skin to have ready for emergencies. The
Administration was absolutely paranoid about safety, but the
arguments and promises of the students had won them over.
And they all knew now that The Tipi breathed fire.

It was almost nine months before the Tipi was reborn in mid-October in a fixed place where it stopped roaming forever. From beginning to end it was a woman's world. It was made by woman from many Departments as well as English 24, Native American Literature. Women's Studies was now part of the curriculum, and many of young feminists joined the Tipi cause. Women in the newly opened Children's Center wanted to bring children. Beth Burkens and Linda Kitz from Women's Studies wanted to use the Tipi for some of their own classes, which lifted a huge psychic burden from me by sharing out the responsibility, and so the work went on. When Kaci finished the outer skin, she had enough canvas left over to make the smoke liner, too.

Many hearts and hands helped locate three dead redwood suckers in the far back part of Cabrillo's property where there was no road. They pushed the suckers down and brought them to the new site to work on, carrying them by hand the whole way. Only two were long enough and straight enough for legs. The third dead redwood sucker was three feet short and too thin to bear the canvas weight. They set it aside to use as one of the Smoke Flap guide poles to direct the wind flow by opening and closing the Smoke Flaps. It was quite a spectacle on the day the canvas was ready to fit. Starting around noon a line of students carried down the rest of the skeleton from their nest on top of the campus. The young pole had finally dried out, but still required seven strong women to carry it down. For hours you could see the lines of students carrying down those 35' tipi poles on their shoulders, one pole at a time, then climbing back up the long hill for more.

In spite of the odds, The People had spoken. On the day the Tipi was erected, wrapped, trimmed, tucked and lined inside and tight on the poles, the Lodge no longer felt out of balance.

When they were finished, we drove in a few stakes to hold

down the skin in case of another big wind, but still gave enough space to lift her skirts on hot days and air the Tipi out.

Properly Prayed for, the born again Tipi was Blessed by Elders from the local Indian TENA Council and a Chumash woman named Chaqueesh, who was teaching a class on Native foods for Cabrillo's Extension and had lived many years at the Santa Barbara Inter-tribal commune headed by a Chumash Elder named Grandfather Semu Huate. Beth Berkins and Linda Kitz were there with members of their own classes, and our small hidden meadow was filled with dozens of happy students and teachers celebrating their Dream Come True.

Many classes, Speakers, and Events occurred in the 'new' Tipi over the next six years, with enough learning problems to fill another book, but two more Mysterious events occurred that stayed with me. The first was when I received a phone call at my home from a former student named Jim, who had taken my first English 1A Class in 1968.

He was totally blind and I hadn't heard from him in years. He said that when he was hanging out at the Rio Del Mar Esplanade two blocks from his house, he overheard two brothers complaining about all the bad luck they kept having since they stole the campus tipi. Jim started talking to them, made friends, and after a few weeks convinced the men that he could lift their curse if they would return the tipi cover to the school. They finally agreed and one of them phoned me a few days later and said I could pick up the tipi in the Rio Del Mar parking lot. I borrowed a friend's old pick up truck and drove right down, hoping to catch and talk to the thieves, but when I arrived the tipi sat in a stinking heap near the entrance to the beach, Over a third of it had been fouled by rat shit, while the rest of the canvas was rank with the smell of mold. I returned the unusable pile of garbage to the Cabrillo Warehouse, where they made me store it in an old shed fifty feet away from the mail building. I filed an Incident report with the Campus Police and that chapter was officially closed.

That's when Brant Segunda, another student from my first Eng. 24 class nearly ten years ago showed up at my office door dressed like Indiana Jones without the whip, carrying a satchel full of Brilliant *Huichole* Yarn Paintings he wanted to show to the class. And boy, did he have a story to tell!

During that first Tipi class one of the students, an elementary school teacher from Watsonville named Juan Carillo, brought a guest named Prem Dass, a bright young California drop out who had been apprenticed to Juan's Grandfather, A shaman named Don Jose, who led annual week long peyote pilgrimages into the Sonora Desert. Prem Dass brought several *Huichole* yarn paintings recording some of their visions. Prem Dass's story deeply impressed Brant, who had been reading the books of Carlos Castaneda before taking English 24.

Brant spoke with Juan after that class and got some general directions about where Don Jose's mountain village might be located, but Juan wouldn't tell precisely. The village location was secret. Period. But Brant had been reading Carlos Castaneda and was obsessed with finding his own Don Juan Spirit Guide. When class was over that semester, Brant dropped out of school and headed south to Ixtlan, Heart of the mountains between Tepic and the sea. Prem Dass told Bent where Jose's grandmother Lupe lived in the town of Tepic, where artists would bring their yarn paintings to sell in the *Mercado*.

Lupe welcomed Brant's visit but refused to disclose her Grandfather's location. So, trusting to his own inner guidance, Brant hiked boldly into the mountains, following what he hoped was a trail to the nearest village. But Brant's internal compass was off. It was also extremely hot and humid and

Brant didn't bring much water or food. After three days and nights of wandering down deer paths, he collapsed from exhaustion and thirst and fell unconscious, still wondering why the mythical Dan Juan hadn't come to his rescue. Left to his own resources, he would have died.

Meanwhile at a nearby village, an elderly Shaman dreamt and saw Brant dying on a little used trail. At dawn he sent his sons down the mountain to find him and bring Brant back up to the village. They did that, and Brant stayed for over a month in the hut of a 115 year old woman Shaman — Great Grandmother of Juan Carillo — who brought him back to health and into a new life.

Soon after recovering, Brant met Juan's Great Grandfather, Don Jose. They adopted Brant into their family, and for the next seven years Brant studied and trained with Don Jose Matsuwa to be a *Mara'akame* (Shaman), learning to pray with feathers, talk in ancient tongues to living gods, and heal with songs and a drum. With Don Jose's blessing, and often with his mentor's company, Brant became a traveling link between the remote village artists and art collectors in the United States.

And Brant brought dozens of yarn paintings which he displayed and interpreted for us around the fire where the colors came alive and danced before our eyes. But Brant's greatest gift of all to us was 105 year old Don Jose Matsuwa himself, who Brant brought with him a year later for a return visit.

Don Jose was a surprise and a delight. He stood about 5' 2" with wrinkled dark skin, wearing an all white outfit with colorful woven designs around the shoulders, waist, and pant legs. His fur-lined white brightly beaded hand-made deerskin boots came over his ankles and disappeared into the flared wide pant legs. His flat white wide brimmed hat was decorated with yarn paintings and feathers. His wide Mayan forehead, broad face and dark mischievous eyes linked him to a race of pyramid builders, mystical Sun worshipers, and creators of empires that ruled the entire American continent from South America through Central America and Mexico for thousands years. Vigorous, mischievous, sparkling with good humor, Don Jose spoke to us in *Hichole*, pausing now and then so Brant could translate.

In a soft voice, Don Jose explained that he had only been studying Shamanism for about ten years when, at the age of 76, he lost his right arm in an explosion while loading cases of dynamite onto a truck. The blast blew him fifty feet back and tore off his right arm. Instead of dying or giving up, which most of us would have done, Don Jose went on to father three more children and doubled down on his study of the arts of healing. He became reclusive but increasingly more cheerful as he grew into his teachings. Now he breathes with the rhythm of nature and tends to his holy Blue Corn plants high on his Sierra mesa on his ranchero. He lives with eagles and sings to the clouds. There are no roads to his house, but he bragged he could still carry 100 pound bags of Blue Corn Meal a mile up the side of the mountain. He said that after the Spanish came, the *Huicholes* and *Coras* and many other tribes had withdrawn to the mountains rather than be murdered, enslaved, and forced to give up their religion, which was based on peyote, rather than be forced to convert to that false, cruel, Spanish god.

Don Jose frequently stays up all night chanting and praying for the welfare of his large, ever expanding family. *"Is your heart happy?"* he asks all of his children at the ranchero. "Dance with all your heart! We are following the example of the gods and the path they have taught us. This is our life!" The Dance of the Deer is truly the path with heart for the *Huicholes*, and Don Jose was a living embodiment of a mythology and world view utterly unlike our own. He wants us to realize the aliveness and beauty of this world and to awaken our sensitivity to our own place within nature. He says that through chanting, drumming, dancing and prayer, we are able to enter trance states which help us 'shift' our consciousness and healings can occur.

Once he was called to a nearby village to minister to a Cora Indian woman who had forgotten her ways — her people's beliefs — which is why she got sick. Don Jose did a ceremony with her and her husband. As he was leaving, he met a priest who had come to give the woman the Last Rites. "You're too late," Don Jose teased the Priest. "She's going to live!" Three days later the woman got up and continued with her life.

Although he hasn't mastered English yet, don Jose speaks Spanish and many dialects from surrounding tribes. He had trained numerous apprentices, including two North Americans — Prem Dass and Brant Segunda — empowering them to hold healing ceremonies in the *Huichole* tradition. Prem Dass married the daughter of a fellow Shaman shortly after Brant began training with Don Jose. In their tradition, Prem Dass changed families, rancheros and teachers. But both groups shared their pilgrimages to *Wirakuta*, that place in the high Sonora Desert where the Peyote tribes grow. A dozen years after we started our journey in Native American Indian Poetry and Prose, Brant had returned to the Cabrillo tipi as an empowered Prayer Leader, and he brought his mentor Don Jose as proof of his diploma.

Brant continues working with the *Huicholes* and has founded The Dance of the Deer Foundation, fostering art from the *Huicholes* and cultural exchange by leading small groups on pilgrimages to sacred places such as Mount Shasta and other sacred spots on the west coast for ceremonies.

Working with Iron Man Mark Allen, Brant published *Fit Soul, Fit Body, 9 Keys to a Healthier Happier You.*

Over the next six years hundreds of students and many great teachers came to the campus tipi and shared living truths with students sitting in a sacred circle. You can not be intimate sitting in long straight lines of chairs separate from each other, everyone facing in one direction with the many forced to listen to one. Round Space affects the mind in a different ways then do squares and boxes. It erases hierarchy. The weathered and wearing lodge loomed large on the lower campus as a viable alternative to "straight thinking", only visible to those who sought it out.

Many native voices, drums, songs, and stories were heard across our sacred tipi fire. Many meetings were for women led by women and I know the Tipi rejoiced in their Beings.

I still remember one stormy night when a tall young Lakota Warrior named Stampede came to urge our attendance at a Red Road Pow Wow to be held that weekend at Indian Camp.

Outside the wind was howling, but Stampede insisted that the weather would be beautiful by tomorrow. He told a wild story of herding Buffalo on his Reservation, and before he finished we could actually hear the terrifying sounds of a thousand Buffalo hooves pounding around the Tipi, followed by powerful flashes of lightning which blew out all the Transformers and plunged the college into darkness. Thirty or more of us remained cozy inside by the fire, secure and dry in our lodge, while outside the dark cold buildings of the campus were evacuated and the parking lots emptied. But we didn't know that until 9:30pm when one of the students who left a little early came running back in the fading rain to warn that there were no lights and the campus seemed abandoned. We ended class and stepped outside into a ghost world. The rain was easing up and smelled fresh and new like back in

BC — Before Columbus! Without electricity, today could be a thousand years ago, and no doubt will be again someday, since nature and time move in circles. According to the First People, We Are Nature. We are Earth People. We are time itself.

8.

Just as time disappears in a tipi so the Coyote Tipi grew old and disappeared into time, The canvas started to rot around the bottom and we were unable to stop it. The Aptos Fire Marshall informed us that the fire retardant in the canvas has worn out and the canvas needed to be replaced. However, the price of canvas had more than doubled since we last checked. Prop.13 had ripped funding from California Schools, leaving public K-14 schools in chaos, starved for cash. "Special" classes like Art and Music and Dance were being slashed. Our Department was told to change it's literature offerings again. Ethnic studies were no longer required.

After more than a dozen years, we collectively agreed to take the Tipi down. The Coyote Tipi story had come full circle. Brant was the seed kernel into whom Jose Carillo had planted brilliant peyote visions at Cabrillo College in our first class meeting when the Tipi was born. Then Don Jose picked up the seeker who fell on his path, and raised him as he did other crops of Anglo and Indigenous Spirit Seeds on his Mountain Ranchero. Finally, the reborn visionary had returned to bless our Cabrillo Garden of Knowledge where our search began.

Ho! Mataquiase! The Coyote Tipi tale is finished!

Tipi Growing, drawing by 7 year old.

Erecting The Coyote Tipi on Cabrillo College's hilltop.

The Coyote Tipi at the peak of it's power.

Brant Secunda & T, Mike Walker in side The Coyote Tipi.

Santa Cruz Mountain Memories
by Daniel Friedman

Part I. Alba Road 1968-70

I first moved to the Santa Cruz mountains in May 1968. After finishing my 3rd year at Reed College in Oregon and a brief visit with my parents, I got a ride to Pacifica and hitchhiked down Highway 1, then up Highway 9. Carrying only what fit into my trusty old Kelty backpack, I walked the last half mile or so to join my companions, Roxane and Terry, at 1000 Alba Road, Ben Lomond.

That property had been the home of a nudist colony known as Eden West. I no longer recall the stories of why or how the colony disbanded, but for the last couple of years the land belonged to a smaller group of people who began to call themselves the New Family. The Family was led by Eric Clough, an architect in his late 40s. I was a bit overawed by that busy benevolent bear of man, but found the others quite approachable, especially Michael, a slender man in his early 30s who was happy to share his vast trove of back-to-the-land lore and skills, and his insights into new-age family dynamics and self-actualization. Matriarch Carol and early-30s Carol also occasionally took us under their wings. We were impressed and inspired by their warm and stable group marriage.

At that time, 1000 Alba Road covered about two sunny acres including a large vegetable garden fenced against the deer, a serious compost pile and chicken coop, a dozen fruit trees, and a deep oval swimming pool thick with green algae. The New Family lived in the main house and rented out a smaller boxy bunkhouse near the property's northern boundary. Somehow Roxane and Terry had managed to become their tenants the previous Fall.

A few words about my companions. Roxane and I had met in high school, at an anti-war weekend gathering in La Honda sponsored by the Quakers' AFSC. About a year later we began an on-again off-again affair. She started college at UC Riverside but transferred to UCSC in Fall 1967. Terry, the younger brother of my high school friend Paul, had begun his pre-med studies at UCSC the previous year. Roxane wanted to try a menage-a-trois. Terry and I had misgivings but were willing to give it a try.

I have fond memories of summer 1968. I slept on a platform suspended from four tall redwood trees. The hillside, at the boundary of 1000 and 1010 Alba, was steep enough that I could walk a nearly level plank out to the 8' x 8' platform, and from the far end look about 30 feet down to lovely Alba Creek. A creekside ram pump occasionally would kick in, ka-thump ka-thump, to send water up to the swimming pool and garden. Nobody wore clothes, just a hat and sandals, except to go into town or on a chilly evening. It only took me a couple of days to get used to it, and soon I too had a nice overall tan.

Terry turned out to be an even better companion than I expected. Incredibly generous and warm, he was (and still is) always looking for ways to make the world a better place. Sometimes he would take me to work alongside his friends in Alan Chadwick's garden at UCSC. I learned to double-dig the clay soil, incorporate compost and leaf mold and crushed limestone, to sow seeds densely and use lots of mulch, in what Alan called the French intensive or biodynamic method. Organic farming in Santa Cruz and beyond was seeded by Alan's apprentices, including Terry's friends Jim and Beth, who founded Camp Joy in Boulder Creek the following year.

Rapid changes came to Alba Road in 1968. I remember Michael telling me the news of Robert Kennedy's assassination in June, and of the New Family's plans to leave the US before it imploded. That future seemed quite plausible, as political chaos descended on many cities following Martin Luther King's assassination and the continuing escalation of the Vietnam war. The New Family put a deposit on a 100+ acre parcel in the Slocan Valley in remote British Columbia, and put 1000 Alba up for sale. Fairly soon they had a buyer connected with Pacific High School, a radical alternative private high school off Skyline Drive. Fortunately by then, the owners of 1010 Alba needed caretakers and offered us the job — free rent in exchange for maintenance and minor repairs and improvements. I kept the platform over Alba Creek.

Our sleeping arrangements were a bit complicated. Taking a cue from the New Family — as I understood it, each day the two Carols decided together where the men would spend the night — Roxane would choose to spend some nights with me on the platform, some with Terry, and occasionally by herself. I don't recall Terry ever complaining about the arrangements, but sometimes I was unhappy. With chagrin, I still remember throwing a tantrum one August afternoon in the Sierra. The three of us got a ride to Mineral King on the west side of the range and backpacked for 10 days, living mainly on rice, oats, fern fiddleheads and trout. Tantrum aside, it was glorious. We hitchhiked back home from Whitney Portal on the east side.

1010 Alba got less sun than 1000, especially in winter, but Terry and I put in a vegetable garden in the sunniest spot, at the end of the driveway, and dug in the last few wheelbarrows of chickenshit from the now-empty coop at 1000 Alba. Once we (and the cat we inherited) got proficient at catching gophers, the garden gave us good harvests, and so did an avocado tree.

It is hard to believe nowadays how little cash was required for a simple life in the late 1960s. Transportation was almost free with Terry's Honda 50 motorcycle that sipped $0.35/ gallon gas, supplemented by hitchhiking. Rent was cheap in the Santa Cruz mountains, and free at 1010 Alba. We grew some of our own food, made yogurt from milk powder, ground all sorts of flour with our Corona mill, and baked lots of bread every week. We traded some of it for eggs with one set of neighbors, and traded it for sand dabs and other bycatch with the fisherfolk down the hill who were especially fond of our challah.

Every couple of months we'd join friends with a van and drive to Oakland's Fruitvale Market to replenish our sacks of rice, garbanzo and kidney beans and wheatberries, and our stocks of gluten flour, milk powder and bulk spices. (Such expeditions later morphed into coops like New Leaf, which later morphed into a small local business that eventually merged with a national chain.) With food stamps in hand, a weekly trip to Ben Lomond Supermarket provided a few luxuries, like ingredients for hand-cranked ice cream. Fees at UCSC were far less than a tenth of what they are now. Until the mid-1970s, jobs were easy to find when we needed cash. A month or two each summer at a union job on the San Francisco waterfront covered my groceries and rent all year.

Our part of Alba Road had a noble tradition of nudity that we tried to uphold. Our hippie visitors were all cool with it, but not all visitors were hippies. For reasons I no longer remember, Sara Bunnett (wife of UCSC Chemistry Department Chair Joe Bunnett) pulled into our driveway one afternoon while I was working nude in the garden. As a matter of principle, I didn't put on any clothes before asking her if she needed help. She quickly backed back up the driveway and disappeared. At numerous social events many years later, Sara's first remark on seeing me would be what a naked savage I had been. Joe would just let it go, and talk shop.

Roxane, Terry and I believed all along that we would need another woman to join and stabilize our menage. My young friend Martha would be perfect — she was adventurous, as upbeat as Terry, and would love life in the Santa Cruz mountains. She was at her parents' home back East that summer, and I didn't have their phone number so I wrote her a long letter of invitation. We never heard back. Sally Muhly, a UCSC local about our age, showed some interest in joining us but then decided against it. In November Terry started spending time in town with Mary, a young UCSC student, and they returned to 1010 most weekends, but it wasn't the same. Our menage had quietly fissioned.

Meanwhile, next door at 1000 Alba, Ken and Patty Kinsey were running a boarding residence for Pacific High School. I had managed to persuade Reed college officials that I needed to spend my senior year at UCSC to write an undergraduate thesis. I found a UCSC sponsor (Marshall Sylvan, the Math Dept's only statistician) and a backdoor for taking all the courses I needed (Concurrent Enrollment via University Extension). I lived a split existence that year, 60% mountain hippie and 40% UCSC undergrad, both parts wonderful in their own way.

Roxane missed her period in December and we decided that, at age 21, we had both matured to the point where we could be good parents. Although in principle opposed to the institution of marriage, we came to appreciate the overwhelming practical benefits. I got a scholarship to begin graduate studies next Fall at UCSC that paid twice as much if I had a wife and child, so Roxane wouldn't have to drop out of school. About then Rabbi Shlomo Carlebach came to campus and we stayed in town that evening. Shlomo began his show in the Merrill dining hall by greeting everyone in person. When he got to me he gazed deep into my eyes and said, "Hi Dan, how are you doing? Flying high?" — he seemed to know my name through means neither of us understood. After the show he agreed to marry us after Roxane converted to Judaism. She was willing, and was a very quick study. We spent several weekends at House of Love and Prayer events in San Francisco and beyond, and Shlomo married us in April in a meadow on Mt Tamalpais, near where the Dipsea Trail begins its final descent to Stinson beach.

Segue

In the Spring, the owners of 1010 Alba decided to sell, and we had to clear out in June. Roxane stayed with her mom in Davis, and I joined Terry and Mary on a month-long road trip. We hitchhiked out to Idaho, and backpacked in the Sawtooth mountains where we lived a few extra days on smoked trout and berries. Back on the road, we spent a night with the Flathead Indians in their reservation, and then rejoined the New Family for a week in Winlaw, BC.

The New Family was thriving. They were making great progress in building their communal farm on raw land while navigating the cultural cross-currents of that time and place. Terry, Mary and I learned about the Doukhobors — an earlier generation of Russian Christian back-to-the land communal nudist utopians — and all sorts of survivalists and ecotopian activists who were gathering in the Slocan Valley. We would all work all day in the fields (or, for most of the women, in the kitchen), and stay up late talking over ideas from Aldo Leopold, EF Schumacher, and other sages who later inspired the Whole Earth Catalog and books like Ecotopia. I added to the mix some 19th century forerunners like Oneida community, Fourier phalanxes, and Owenites as well as ongoing Israeli kibbutzim.

In late July 1969, we returned to the Bay Area. With me by her side in San Francisco's enlightened French Hospital, Roxane gave birth to our son Aryeh on August 16, a bit early. We (Roxane, Aryeh and I; Terry and Mary; our geologist friend Barry; and one or two others) found a large house in Cave Gulch to fix up and lease. It was perfect: definitely in the Santa Cruz mountains but less than a 15 minute deer trail scramble to my grad student office in the UCSC Math department. Unfortunately, our lease gave the owner the option to sell the house before Thanksgiving, which he did, barely. Roxane and I had to move into town, where we found a nice little house on Pelton Ave, on lower west side of town. We lived there for a year.

Before recounting our return to the mountains, let me tie a few loose ends. Alba Road addresses were drastically renumbered at some point, and the properties I mentioned are now around 10870 Alba. Ralph Abraham tells me that the Pacific High School affiliated owner of 1000 Alba was Bob Spitzer, a Palo Alto psychiatrist. 1010 Alba ultimately was purchased by UCSC Math professor Harold Widom, who rented out to my classmate Bobby Dubinsky and his wife Peggy and young daughter.

In 1972, my young friend Martha's older sister wrote me a long letter explaining that their mother, who regarded me as a bad influence, had intercepted my invitation letter and never let Martha see it. But not long after, before her 20th birthday, Martha died suddenly at home of a cerebral hemorrhage. Her sister told me that Martha had deeply enjoyed her time with me and thought that she would have loved trying life in the Santa Cruz mountains. Sally Muhly also died before her time, perhaps around 2001.

Science Fiction legend Robert Heinlein was a longtime friend of Eric Clough and, I'm told, sometimes hung out with the New Family. I think Heinlein's recurrent themes of nudism and group marriage were inspired by the New Family and its predecessors, but it may be a coincidence that the hero of his epic Stranger in a Strange Land had almost the same name as our one-time neighbor, Michael Valentine Smith.

Part II. Lompico, 1971-74

Roxane and I lived comfortably in town but missed the mountains and wanted to raise our son there. By early 1971 I had made enough progress as a grad student and had enough savings to think about buying a modest mountain parcel. Tony Tromba, a new addition to the Math Dept faculty, was also interested in buying land so we joined forces. After a search, we settled on a new subdivision high on a ridge above Zayante, accessible by roads through Lompico. Tony bought 12 ridgetop acres with a stunning view of lower San Lorenzo valley and the ocean beyond the Santa Cruz Boardwalk. My 6 acre parcel lay just below, near the west end of the subdivision, facing southeast.

My parents filled a gap between my savings and the $5,000 down payment, and gave us their largest umbrella tent. I pitched it on a level patch near the bottom of the property and we moved in around March 1. Winter was not yet done that year, and Roxane, Aryeh and I often had to bring our Coleman stove inside the tent to cook dinner. Part of my graduate student support package was teaching abstract math to Pajaro Valley elementary school kids, and I had use of a university car to get there and back. One morning the car got stuck on our muddy dirt road and after winching it out and driving to South County I had just enough time to change my shirt but not my shoes and pants. Someone from the Principal's office complained about my appearance, but fortunately the UC folks who were funding the operation noted my success in reaching the students and merely requested that I take care to avoid further complaints.

Anticipating lots of hauling, I bought a 1952 Ford pickup truck, complete with compound low gear, for $75 and a blender; we had gone off-grid and so had no use for electric appliances. The truck's recent coat of purple house paint was already beginning to peel. I later heard that its previous owners were anxious to disguise and unload following a bad drug deal somehow involving that truck. Anyway, the Ford Motor Company back in the early 1950s made simple, sturdy engines and transmissions, and with a bit of coaching from skilled friends, I was able to keep the truck running pretty well.

By May, if memory serves, we found someone willing to sell us the second-hand components of a geodesic dome: two pickup loads of 1x2x30" wooden equilateral triangles covered with blue and green 10mil vinyl sheets, enough to assemble into a 26' diameter 3/8 sphere. I cleared and partly leveled a site halfway up the slope from our tent. Lots of our friends came by on a Saturday, and by nightfall we had a dome home, with a dirt floor, trapezoidal front door, two triangular screened openable windows and a large adjustable pentagonal top vent. We built a bonfire outside and partied late into the evening.

In following weeks, I managed to set up a wood stove inside the downhill edge of the dome, and built a loft above shelves and kitchen counter, just below the top vent. Just inside the dome's uphill edge I put in hinged storage structures forming a long curved window seat. The dome was becoming quite livable, but eventually the floor dried out and became too dusty for our toddler. I managed salvage a full truckload of scrapped 2x6 tongue-and-groove mill-ends from Big Creek lumber for (as I recall) about $30. Together with a couple of salvaged 2x10 joists, they allowed me to create a split-level paved interior — a real boost to our standard of living!

Roxane and I had purchased a dozen mail-order fertilized eggs, supposedly all hens-to-be, and hatched them shortly before we moved to the mountains. By April we realized that we had three roosters. The noisy alpha and beta roosters happily did their jobs of fertilizing the nine hens, but they all picked on the timid gamma rooster, who eventually refused to return at night to the sturdy small coop I built. One night a raccoon got him, leaving only a few feathers and body parts. The alpha and beta then had more battles, and I could see no reason to keep them both, so beta became a hearty chicken stew. A few weeks later, the alpha rooster decided to show toddler Aryeh who was boss, and pecked him in the eye. After we returned from the emergency room (good news, no lasting harm done!), rooster alpha also became stew. The remaining hens were bait for raccoons and an occasional bobcat, and laid fewer eggs as they aged. By the time we were down to the final four hens, they were not worth the trouble. Lots of chicken stew the next month.

A goat was our only other adventure in animal husbandry. The idea was to help clear the poison oak and other underbrush, and to provide milk for Aryeh who didn't do well on cow's milk. At our budget, the goat ranch offered us only one goat, named Semolina. Perhaps slightly traumatized by the pickup truck ride to our place, she bahhed mournfully for weeks. She was happy with the oats and high end feed we gave her, nibbled some poison oak, and gave us a quart or so of milk every day. But Semolina always seemed lonely, and it was a real burden to feed and milk her every day. So after a year or so, we gave her back to the goat ranch.

Our six acre parcel was mostly forested, with lots of oak and madrone and hundreds of 6-30" diameter redwood trunks sprouting densely from stumps of old-growth trees logged 70 or 80 years earlier. I cleared space for a modest vegetable garden in the sunniest spot, near the parcel's western edge, and just a bit uphill, near the top of the property, another space for a cabin. That required felling about twenty trees; out of respect, for that purpose I used only a bow saw. I had no compunctions about using borrowed chainsaws to buck the logs for firewood, which became my main trade good. I parlayed it into a kitchen sink, a propane-powered refrigerator, and many other amenities.

Our nearest on-the-grid neighbors were Tim and Jan who, along with Jan's young kids, rented a house a five minute walk west of the dome. They were very generous in taking phone messages for us and otherwise supporting our homesteading effort. So were Art and Jeannine Swafford, and older couple who lived further around the ridge towards Lompico. We became friends with others who bought parcels in the subdivision, including Pierre and Julie Bourriague at the eastern end of the ridgetop, who quickly built themselves a modern home featuring lots of heavy beams and glass. A commune occupied two parcels down the hill from them, with several couples and half a dozen kids living in trailers and tented platforms; the only names I still recall are Steve and Eva Kirsch, who were about our age and had a kid arrive the next year.

By midsummer 1971 we were starting to plan our own dreamhouse, inspired by books on Japanese architecture and books and back-to-the land articles by Ken Kerns and other contributors to Mother Earth News. I sketched a pole frame house with removable wall panels on two sides, opening to a wrap-around cantilevered porch, and an overhanging roof with a south facing clerestory window and roof/deck. That Fall

I thinned some of the multiple-trunk stumps, and gathered a dozen 18-24" diameter redwood trunks for the structural poles. I spent several tedious winter days trying to dig a 3x4 array of 6' deep holes 10' apart in a gentle but rocky slope. Fortunately John Lingemann (the younger, only a couple of years older than me) had a rig nearby to drill a well to supply water for the subdivision. His rig took only an hour or two to do the remaining 75% of the job.

For the floor beams and roof beams I felled some slightly smaller redwood trunks, and (after they dried a few months) cut them down the middle with a hand-held chainsaw. I brought in pickup loads of sand and gravel and bags of Portland cement. I dumped a large barrowload of wet concrete into each hole, and the next day set the poles. Then, using a chalkline and level, I drilled holes with a brace and bit, and bolted the half-round floor beams to the poles.

About that time, some anonymous person reported my unpermitted construction to the County. If memory serves, it was my neighbor Pierre who put me in touch with Kastutis Dovydaitis, a nuclear power plant engineer with a guilty conscience. He lent me his drafting table and helped me prepare official blueprints for my cabin. He submitted signed calculations noting that the structure would withstand an earthquake stronger than ever recorded in the US. The County approved the design after a couple of months, but insisted that I install a septic leach field instead of the composting toilet I had in mind. (Perhaps all my lobbying had a delayed effect, since a year or two later the County trumpeted its progressive thinking on composting toilets!) The septic field cost about $2000 to install, essentially doubling the out-of-pocket cost of my cabin.

In August, all the half-round redwood beams were ready and I had purchased all the necessary 2x8 joists and bolts, so

I sent out invitations for a roof-raising on a Saturday. Most of my neighbors came, along with a few more distant friends from town. Drawing on everyone's equipment and skills, we hoisted up and bolted on all the roof beams and set most of the roof and floor joists. An hour before sundown, we put down all the drills and chisels, made a campfire in the garden clearing, and ate, drank and partied long into the night.

Life didn't slow for all this construction. Terry had moved to Hawaii to begin medical school. While completing her undergrad studies, Roxane became increasingly involved in the women's health collective, then led by Kate Boland and our former Alba Road neighbor Patty, now called Raven Lang. That fall, Roxane decided to separate from me and live in town.

I soon found people to share the land and to help with mortgage payments and construction. Chris and Patty moved into the umbrella tent below. Apprentice carpenter Chuck slept on a platform not far from the dome. Mark, a 40-ish martial arts fanatic, pitched his teepee near the eastern edge of my parcel. Michelle, a stunning 17-year-old, stayed with us while finishing up at San Lorenzo HS. That Fall and Winter, I'd generally return from town on Thursday evening, and we'd all gather in the dome, eat dinner (usually vegan, usually prepared by Patty), then often smoke one of Chris's hash-oil spiked joints and philosophize and maybe try to plan the next few days. Chuck's musician friends sometimes joined us for the weekend. On Tuesday morning, I'd go back to town and campus.

Gradually, gradually, the cabin came together. We built an interior fireplace with two pickup loads of red brick and yellow fire brick salvaged from a long-abandoned limestone kiln in Bonny Doon, and with a fire jacket/smoke shelf I welded under the guidance of a friend of a friend and a Ken

Kern design. A thermocouple-powered fan blew air past the heat jacket and through side vents to heat the whole cabin. Richard, a sometime grad student of elephant seal wizard Burney Le Boeuf and a member of the Felton Guild commune, showed me how to make professional-grade kitchen cabinets at the Guild's facilities. By late summer 1972 I had moved from the dome to the cabin and began to winterproof it. Using only hand tools on rough-cut 2x4s and irregular siding, it took a while to finish and fit the removable panels, but it was sooo satisfying to install the last panels and windows and thereby terminate kitchen raids by local squirrels and raccoons.

The cabin accommodated up to a dozen guests accustomed to hippie hospitality. Many out-of-town visitors oohed and aahed at the way the dark redwood bark of the interior structural poles set off the blonde tongue-and-groove fir floorboards (a bit of a splurge). The floors, ceiling and walls were all well insulated so the central fireplace kept the whole place warm in the evening, and the wood stove helped draw everyone to the kitchen in the morning. One snowy weekend we had three amateur guitarists playing entire songbooks of Paul Simon, Joni Mitchell, Bob Dylan while the rest of us sang along.

About that time, Shaney and Rebecca became our new neighbors, with plans to build their dream house on the parcel between mine and that rented by Tim and Jan. They were a bit older than us, with a successful business over the hill, and boundless energy and enthusiasm for mountain life.

Coda

My mountain time was running out faster than I realized. For 1972-73 I got a prestigious scholarship to teach an original undergraduate course and to travel to write my dissertation, along with word that no further support could be expected. So, despite unfinished interior walls, in March 1973 I rented out my cabin and hitchhiked to Cambridge Massachusetts, and worked as hard as I could with mathematician John Guckenheimer. He encouraged me to develop my idea for using Trotter products to solve reaction-diffusion systems that could ultimately explain such things as how embryos develop spatial structures and organs from an initially uniform sphere of cells. But in the end, my idea didn't work.

At that point I needed to find a job that could help pay for my son Aryeh's medical care. He was missing milestones, like walking and toilet training and talking, but his conditions were hard to diagnose. So I took a computer-intensive job in Berkeley, and later started teaching math at College of Marin. Just before Thanksgiving 1974 my tenant in Lompico phoned from Tim and Jan's house — while he was in town, my cabin had mysteriously burned to the ground! Earthquakes couldn't touch it, but it had no defense against flames when nobody was there to operate the fire extinguishers.

That ended my hopes of returning to my mountain home. At my father's insistence, I had fire insurance, and the adjuster offered a payment that returned less than $2/hr for the time I put into it. I took the offer, sold the land to a Vietnam vet named Warren.

My life was changing quickly. I found my life partner, Penny, while I was taking my last shot at finishing my PhD. This time, under the supervision of eminent Berkeley mathematician Stephen Smale, my idea worked and after 6 months of intensive writing I submitted my dissertation, which used dynamical systems theory to study the stability of economic systems. Penny and I got married and later, using the money from Warren and the insurers, we bought and fixed up a rundown Victorian house in North Oakland. After two years in industry (a story in its own right!) and several years as assistant professor of economics at UCLA, in 1985 I got an offer to join the economists at UCSC. I couldn't resist returning to Santa Cruz, now joined by Penny and our kids Sara (then 4) and Ben (2). We first looked for a house in Cave Gulch, but none was on offer. So we bought a wonderful distressed old farmhouse on the lower west side of town, and fixed it up. We still live there.

Pierre, Julie, Shaney and Warren still live in their same mountain homes, but of course they are all now senior citizens. I no longer dream of back-to-the-land self sufficiency, and no longer have the quick deep connection with other such dreamers. I enjoy life and work in town, and walks on West Cliff, but it only takes a whiff of Yerba Buena or a glimpse of blooming Ceanothus to trigger memories of my mountain homestead.

Aryeh in Dome, 1971

Cabin Construction, 1971

Life is a Stage: Audrey Stanley Directs
by Don Monkerud

Since its rebirth after the founding of UCSC, Santa Cruz became the home of many accomplished and independent voices, including Audrey Stanley. Her love for Shakespeare began early. Selected in the first drama class at the University of Bristol in England, she went on to found the Dramatic Society Touring company and received the first Ph.D. awarded at UC/Berkeley. UCSC was lucky to appoint her as a Professor of Theater Arts. Her production of *Winter's Tale* in 1975 at the Oregon Shakespeare Festival in Ashland became the first directed by a woman. Her efforts in founding the Santa Cruz Shakespeare Festival led to 40,000 attending plays each summer outdoors among the towering redwoods in an informal, relaxed atmosphere. In retirement, she joined the Board of Directors for Shakespeare Santa Cruz at its new location in DeLaveaga Park and enjoyed many performances before passing away in 2022 at age 94.

In 2000, I had the pleasure of interviewing her for a proposed national book, *The Spirit of Santa Cruz: Creativity in a California Community*. Unfortunately, editors didn't see the local/national connection, and the story sat on my computer. She read and approved the following profile.

At times the city on the hill sits separate, isolated, and even estranged from the city below, the actual city, the city of today, of families, of the requirements of get-up-and-go-to-work people. But at other times, the two come together to recognize that each requires the other to maintain a balanced and energized community.

Nowhere is the coming together of the university and the town more evident than in the establishment of the Summer Shakespeare Festival. Few engaged more deeply or gave more

of themselves toward establishing the festival than Audrey
Stanley, a founding member of the Theater Arts Department
at UCSC. With assistance from actors and staff, the university
and the town produced the first plays. They nurtured them
until they took flight and became recognized throughout the
country for their vivacious, creative, and at times unorthodox
performances.

Audrey's circuitous route to Santa Cruz came from her
love of theater. Born in London in the late 1920s, Audrey
faired poorly in the pea soup fog, so poorly that the family
doctor suggested they go to the seashore for her health. In
1929, the family moved to the coastal town of Whitstable. Her
parents met in the Boy Scouts and Girl Guides in England,
married after W.W.I., and moved to Canada in the early 1920s.
Canadian companies had little need for her father's electrical
engineering skills, and the family stopped in New York on the
way back to England. Their landlady greeted them warmly and
volunteered to babysit Audrey's sister while her father took
a job with Otis Elevator. After four years, her mother left the
extreme cold and heat of New York, and her father's mother
bought into a public house, better known as a pub, in London
and asked her father to come back and run it. Nine months
after they returned to London, Audrey was born. Ironically
she narrowly missed being born an American citizen

Although she was a sickly child, Audrey recalls her early
childhood fondly. Her father was athletic and helped train
his two daughters in several sports. When she was young,
her mother had worked in a tea factory and a hat and bonnet
shop, but after she married and moved to Whitstable, she
became politically active, serving on the local city council.
As a founding member of the local Town Women's Guild, she
practiced theater arts and civic studies. She commuted by
train to a nearby Faversham to attend grammar school, where

Audrey's more formal theater education began.

"We had several enterprising literature teachers who took us on the 6:30 milk train to London to the theater," says Audrey. "We got to see Lawrence Olivier, Alec Guinness, and Sir John Gielgud at the Old Vic Theater. My parents started taking me to the theater when I was five. My father bought a box, and we saw British pantomimes like *Mother Goose, Jack and the Bean Stalk, Cinderella, and Aladdin.*"

Audrey formed a theater group by the age of eight and performed a play about a prince and princess in huts on the beach. She directed and played the wicked witch and recalled being somewhat disappointed when the proceeds, the mighty sum of five shillings, were donated to the Children's Hospital, giving her an early view of the business of theater. It took her several years to write her first play, which she completed when she was eleven. W.W.II interrupted her idyllic childhood.

Americans forget that the war began in England in 1939, and by the time the Blitz came, children had been moved to the English countryside or Canada. The Germans bombed and machine-gunned the train running by Audrey's house, the same one she took to school every day. Her mother refused to evacuate her to Canada, opting instead to keep the family together. Everyone participated in the war effort, so Audrey became a bicycle messenger at age twelve and later volunteered at the town's Civic Restaurant. Her father joined the Royal Observer Corp. to spot planes, her mother worked in the Red Cross, and her older sister joined Sir John's Ambulance and went to work in the London bomb shelters. Bombs fell on either side of her house, and although the windows shattered, her house didn't receive a direct hit.

"I was brought up during the war in a very restricted area," explains Audrey. "We had to carry identity cards, and the sea was mined on the beach where we lived. I remember seeing the soldiers coming from Dunkirk. The train was late to take us home from school, and hundreds of us were waiting when another train suddenly came in very slowly from the opposite direction. The train was full of soldiers who looked like ghosts; they were still covered with the dust of battle. They were profoundly moving."

Despite the war, Audrey continued her education, studying Shakespeare and participating in drama competitions where she played Shylock, among other roles. She attended a girls' school where art and humanities were critical in the curriculum. Audrey recalls attending a conference of world leaders toward the end of the war, where she developed strong attitudes supporting a one-world view. She also disliked examinations that separated students into different education tracks, but overall, she enjoyed her school years.

"My funny little private preparatory school was splendid," she says. "It was very small, with only a few students and separate from the boys. We studied algebra and French at an early age. We took exams in a wonderful way, answering questions and moving up the line. We had a lot of fun, and art was my favorite subject."

Audrey remained in high school for an additional year to prepare for university and won entrance to Oxford, which had a backlog of eligible students due to the war. She would have to wait. She refused special treatment from a friend who could pull strings to get her admitted to Oxford earlier and instead selected Bristol University, where she studied French, English Literature, and Drama. Bristol offered the first drama major in a British university (universities were beginning to recognize drama as an academic subject), and Audrey remained an additional year to become one of the first six students to graduate in drama from a British university.

While in the drama program, she was appointed as one

of the two selectors of plays for the National Union of Students Drama Festival, became president of the university theatrical society, and formed a university theater company with 20 other students. She directed *Taming of the Shrew* and took it on the road in western England. She recalls the townspeople in a small village bringing their own chairs to the performance. The French government invited the group to perform in a German youth camp, and when they arrived to perform, the sets hadn't arrived as promised. They came in at the last minute and were passed overhead by the crowd. Two members of the troupe went on to become professional actors in England.

Audrey credits the time at Bristol as reinforcing many of her attitudes about women's rights that her mother, a Labor Party supporter in a very conservative area, taught her. At Bristol, the powerful students' union selected male and female student body co-presidents and each rotated chairing meetings. After visiting Oxford, she realized "that was not the way the world was run." An earnest student, she devoted her time to theater and didn't have time for dating.

By the age of sixteen, Audrey knew she preferred directing to acting. "I just decided I didn't want to be an actress since I couldn't decide who I was," she explains. "Acting like someone else wouldn't help. I suppose it was normal teenage angst, but I made up for my lack of acting knowledge later."

At Bristol, she studied at the Bristol Old Vic Theater School, one of the major repertory companies in England. Special arrangements allowed her to take acting classes while working on her teaching credential. Her goal became to learn more about acting to inform her directing. Upon graduating from Bristol, she spent a year teaching high school in Yorkshire, where she directed in a newly remodeled eighteenth-century theater. Her hopes were dashed when the fire department closed the theater shortly after she arrived. Next, Guilford's experimental school of art hired her to establish drama in the curriculum. Audrey taught drama classes, held improvisational workshops, and directed and acted with London Theater groups.

After living on her savings for six months to write plays and poetry, Audrey worked at a teachers' college in Nottinghamshire, where she taught teachers how to teach drama and produce plays. She spent five years there before moving to a larger department in Birmingham. Then disaster struck. During a freezing winter, Audrey awoke in her unheated room, unable to move. Eventually, she rolled out of bed to turn on her portable heater, but upon visiting the doctor, she discovered the cause of her discomfort was sciatica. The doctor warned that stress would increase her pain. Her job was too stressful, and she became crippled with pain.

"I decided I had to change my life," Audrey explains. "I chucked my job, even though I was offered a principal lectureship. Then a letter came from Dalhousie University in Nova Scotia, Canada, offering a job setting up and teaching a new drama department. I gave up my job and left for Canada."

Her interest in Greek and Roman theaters in Greece, Turkey, Sicily, and Italy motivated her to move. She had taken a class at Bristol by Professor H.D.F. Kitto to study Greek drama. She began visiting the sites and filming theaters. Once she began teaching, she had no time for anything else, and her study of Greek theater languished. She hoped that teaching at a university would allow her to spend more time researching and organizing the material from the 70 ancient Greek theaters she captured on film.

She and another Brit found themselves organizing and planning the four-year drama curriculum for Dalhousie

University, although she knew little about Canadian theater.
To increase her knowledge, she traveled across Canada on
her Christmas break. During the trip, she stopped to see
friends at UC Berkeley and UCLA. In Berkeley, she discovered
a six-month program in classic Greek drama in honor of
founding the first Western Drama Festival 2500 years earlier.
She discussed her film project with the program director, and
he agreed not only to accept her in the Greek program but
also to send her to UCLA to study film, which was part of her
dissertation.

Audrey spent 1966 to 1969 in Berkeley, absorbed in theater
and two quarters at UCLA studying film. She devoted her
time in Berkeley to study and research and completed her
M.A. and Ph. D. in Drama (the first Ph.D. in the program).
During summer break, she acted in three different university
repertory company plays, which became her introduction to
Berkeley's scholar/director concept, which she adopted as her
own.

"The 1960s were a transformational time," she recalls. "As
an older person going back to school was a privilege, and
being in Berkeley where the issues were discussed was special.
I went on marches even though I was on a J1 visa and could
have been deported. I couldn't take time off and get caught
up in political issues as much as I would have liked because
I had no money and wasn't allowed to work due to my visa.
We did produce a play called *Vietnam*. The director thought
I wouldn't be attacked because of my English accent, so I
interviewed people about what they thought about Vietnam,
and we used the recordings in the play."

During her first year in the Berkeley drama program,
Audrey began a special project that would prove enormously
relevant in setting up the Shakespeare Festival at UCSC. As
part of her training as a scholar/director, she realized the

importance of archives to document play productions. Her professor assigned her to research the Ashland, Oregon, Shakespeare Festival play archives. Although she had no idea where Ashland was, let alone Oregon, she traveled to Ashland and met Angus Bowmer, the founder of the Oregon Shakespeare Festival. He gave her the keys to the theater and told her where she could find the prompt books that contained records of the festival's plays that began in the 1930s.

"The prompt books are what the stage manager uses to run the show," she explains. "They record all the moves, the sound effects, the lighting, and other staging requirements. You can recreate a production from the prompt books. Angus Bowmer let me take the prompt books as long as I promised to return them. I got all the programs and researched all the newspapers for reviews. This was marvelous training for setting up the Shakespeare Festival in Santa Cruz."

After graduating from Berkeley in 1969, Audrey applied to teach at Stanford and UCSC, and both accepted her. She chose UCSC due to the university's views on education, including the written evaluations, which she claims are the only way to grade art courses, and its size — there were only 3000 students. Additionally, Dean McHenry insisted on spelling theater with an "er" rather than an "re" to emphasize the theater that is part of mainstream American life, which also delighted Audrey. Along with four or five newly appointed colleagues, including Michael Warren in the English Literature Department and a former president of the Shakespeare Association of America, she helped set up the Board of Studies in Theater Arts at UCSC.

In 1975 she was asked to direct *The Winter's Tale* in Ashland, a memorable production in which she staged the final scene in all white, emphasizing the magical, spiritual side of the play. The final scene ends with Hermione rising from a

Grecian kiosk as if she were a waxen figure who slowly comes back to life. "I wanted to create a sense of having a second chance at reconciliation and forgiveness," she says. "The spiritual values of the play really worked."

The play worked so well that C. L. Barber, a nationally recognized Shakespeare scholar and dean of UCSC Arts and Humanities, saw the play several times. It evidently caught his fancy, for when Audrey returned to UCSC, Barber suggested setting up a graduate program leading to a Shakespeare festival. Because the Theater Arts department also contained film and dance, the idea didn't gain support. The festival had to wait for several more years. Its birth can be traced to a letter in 1980 from Dane Archer, a professor of social science, who asked the chancellor to honor his teacher, C. L. Barber, who had just passed away, with a Shakespeare Festival. They called a meeting of those interested from the town and the university. Since Audrey was already directing *The Tempest* for the Berkeley Shakespeare Festival, someone suggested bringing the play to UCSC. The Berkeley management said it would be too expensive, and the town people made an alternative suggestion: "Let's have our own festival."

"A committee was formed in 1980, and I reluctantly joined, although I knew the prospect would completely take over my life and interrupt my directing elsewhere," recalls Audrey. "But there it was, and it grew from there."

In 1980, during the formation of Shakespeare Santa Cruz, the group brought Tony Church and four other actors from Britain's Royal Shakespeare Company to teach classes and perform for a week. The actors participated in *A Renaissance Triumph*, held at Bargetto's Winery, the first event of Shakespeare Santa Cruz. Michael Warren, a professor of literature at UCSC and president of the Shakespeare Association of America, wanted to do *King Lear*, the 600-word longer folio text, complete and uncut. If they did a tragedy, they also needed a lighter play and chose *A Midsummer Night's Dream*, which Audrey had directed and taken on tour to 16 colleges in California in 1980.

Before committing to a full-blown festival, the newly formed Shakespeare Santa Cruz held a prototype festival in May 1981, featuring the Will Geer Theatricum Botanicum of Los Angeles with Geer's daughter, Ellen Geer, directing *The Taming of the Shrew*. Two performances played in the quarry in modern dress with whips and a leather and chains motif. A truck even drove onto the stage. Kristin Bolder Froid became the paid coordinator for the festival. Audrey attributes the plays' success to the communities' support at a time when eleven different theater groups downtown vied for attention. The prototype season proved there was an audience, and Audrey realized that she could draw on a wide variety of talented actors in the community to support the festival in its initial seasons.

Because they were doing *King Lear* indoors, they decided to do *A Midsummer Night's Dream* outdoors. But where? Audrey performed her 1980 production of the play in the meadow between the library and the performing arts building but everyone roasted in the sun. They needed a cool, shady location. Three people claim to have discovered the Glen — George Kovach, Norvid Roos, and Bonnie Showers — but Audrey thinks it was simultaneous: they were all together when they chanced on the perfectly-worked spot. The audience moved between the Glen and the theater in the first two years before the audience became too large. During its days in the redwoods, the university required that they return the area to pristine condition following the festival.

"The Glen is magical, and the university wants it restored, which means sets must be rebuilt each year with seating in slightly different places," Audrey comments. "We fought a big battle to keep the theater in the Glen from becoming too fixed. When theater gets set in its shape, it's no longer as vital. It just becomes a show."

That first year, Bonnie Showers and George Kovach, the former director of the Berkeley Shakespeare Festival, directed *A Midsummer Night's Dream*. Tony Church played *King Lear*, and Julian Curry played the fool. Dana Evans, an America Equity actor, played Goneril and Kate Hawley played Regan, while pre-professionals and assorted local actors filled the other roles. Novid Roos was the festival designer and provided stage designs. Elain Yokoyama Roos organized the costume shop and designed the costumes for King Lear.

The Chancellor had just married Karen Sinshemimer, who had worked at Twentieth Century Fox, and Audrey asked her to help with the festival by serving on the Board of Directors. The board and the university raised $80,000, which paid for the first festival season and encouraged everyone to continue for a second year.

Audrey lined up Michael Edward, a new faculty director for Theater Arts and UCLA MFA graduate, to direct *Merry Wives of Windsor* and Julian Curry, who played Rumpole of The Bailey on a British TV comedy, to play *Macbeth*. Although community actors, who were only available at night due to their day jobs, limited rehearsal time to three weeks, the plays met with success. Children were drawn in during the second year with a preparatory workshop of Renaissance games and performances in the Santa Cruz Library and the Duck Pond Theater. The festival was off and running, with Audrey contributing as the artistic director for six years and continuing to serve on the board of directors.

"Change is vital to the theater because it needs renewal," she says. "In England, artistic directors moved from one theater to another as they worked their way to the West End in London. In six years, a director is able to establish a vision and provide a fresh impetus to a theater. After that, it's time to bring in someone new."

The festival brought in talented and creative artistic directors. Michael Edward followed Audrey and went on to direct opera in New York and Melbourne, and Sidney, Australia. Danny Scheie, a UC Berkeley Ph.D. who graduated from the same program as Audrey, stirred controversy for what some considered his outlandish emphasis on gender-bending. Audrey points out that he brought in a much younger crowd. Paul Whitworth, an artistic director, came from the Royal Shakespeare Company of London and joined the festival in 1984 to play Prince Hal, a memorable performance on a motorbike when he dressed as Boy George. Audrey continued to sit in on rehearsals with the various directors when they let her.

After teaching for forty years, Audrey retired in 1991 but continued to work with the festival and lend support when requested. Although she never married — her first love always remained the theater — she became the godmother to an English friend's son. Upon her friend's death, the boy attended UCSC before attending Cambridge University. Today she enjoys her role as a grand goddaughter. After retiring, Audrey wrote a series of plays inspired by a Van Gogh exhibit she saw in 1984. She took a summer off from the festival in 1988 and wrote the first play on the relationship between Vincent Van Gogh and Paul Gauguin but put it aside until she could devote more time to the project, which would become a trilogy.

She worked on the third play first, and after several revisions, the local Actor's Theater performed a reading of *Voyages*. She did the same with the trilogy's first play, *The Vow*, and combined the first and second plays as *The Vow and the Visit*, which won third place in the Actor's Theater play competition in 2000. She continued to rewrite the play entitled, *Call me Vincent* and send it to publishers. She decided to archive the early years of the Santa Cruz Shakespeare Festival before they became lost to time and collected materials for the archives housed at UCSC. Even in retirement, the theater remained primary to her. She reminisced on her years of devotion to theater in Santa Cruz as a life well spent.

"It's absolutely amazing to see what we have created," she says. "For this to happen locally says something about the caliber of interest, talent, and energy in the community. It wasn't for nothing that the festival started here, and it couldn't have happened without the combination of the university's and the community's support and interest."

Hip Santa Cruz: SLV Memory
by Nona Williams

I grew up in the Ozark foothills on a remote 75 acre parcel of land that had once been part of the homeland of the great Osage Nation, a Siouan people. When oil was discovered on Osage land in Oklahoma, each enrolled member received a share of that income and some used the funds to return to their Ozark homelands and purchase land.

Our home was located on a dirt road about four miles from the tiny town of Winona. Our house was situated on a hill about a quarter mile up an unpaved driveway. Our only water source was a cistern that collected rainwater. We used a hand pump in the kitchen where we heated the water on our propane stove. We had no plumbing.

A herd of wild horses regularly visited our unfenced pasture land. A trail behind our house led down the hill to a pond and beyond. My dad regularly walked that trail and collected arrowheads. Our location was so remote, no neighbors were visible from our house. When I wasn't at the pond or walking the trail, I was reading a book from the bookmobile at school.

In 1968 my sister and I heard that something interesting was happening in California so we packed up and drove across the country, arriving first in Los Angeles where we experienced an eye-popping amount of big city culture shock. Soon acid trips, cannabis and hippies made us feel welcome. On one occasion, I accidentally joined a demonstration to free Huey Newton when a group of marchers chanted, "Off the sidewalk, into the street!" I joined them and asked someone why we were marching. I hadn't heard of Huey Newton or his cause until then.

In the early 1970s, my sister moved to Santa Cruz County and rented a tiny cabin from Doug and Margo in the Zayante area. Doug was a member of a local group called the Dirty Butter Jug Band and we discovered the Zayante Club where we attended concerts by Jill Croston (aka Lacy Dalton) and a band called Highwire. During the days, visitors lounged around the Zayante Club's swimming pool where clothes were optional.

In 1976 I'd had enough of big city life in Los Angeles so I moved to Santa Cruz and enrolled at Cabrillo College where I signed up for T. Mike Walker's English 1A class. It was a wonderful class and the teacher was amazing. I learned much more than English literature in that class. The reading list included many books by Native American authors and the classes were held outdoors on the grass and under the sun. I met a number of interesting people at Cabrillo.

I soon discovered people with whom I'd had some contact in Los Angeles had also moved to Santa Cruz.

In Los Angeles about 1970 or 1971, Janus Aurah Karma, a colorful woman, had approached my car while I was stopped at a traffic light and handed a paper to me outlining her thoughts on life, the universe and everything. Not long after I moved to Santa Cruz, I saw her on the Pacific Garden Mall sharing her work. She styled herself as a "Universal Messenger".

In October 1976, an article about Natasha Faust and her children Frey and Freya appeared in the Good Times weekly newspaper. I had attended open house meetings at her home in Los Angeles where poets shared their works and activists planned events while discussing worthy causes. Later she and her children performed at the "Theater of Magic" in Ben Lomond.

Another coincidence from my time in Los Angeles was with my neighbor Tiran Porter. One day, on his way out, he told me he was going to an audition and I wished him luck. Later, he left a note on my car thanking me for "the good karma and smiles." and he let me know that he got the job with the Doobie Brothers. Later, I discovered that he and his band were in the San Jose area. It seemed as though I was one of several who had joined the migration north from Los Angeles.

On May 22, 1977, I was invited to attend a peyote ceremony at the Harmony Hill site in Ben Lomond. Parking was limited so we left our cars in the parking lot of The People's Bakery (where Casa Nostra Restaurant is located now). Someone picked us up in a van and ferried us to the Harmony Hill site. Freedom, Crystal, Lone Wolf, Malcolm, Sharon, Dennis, Elizabeth, Peyote Woman (Chela) and others were there. Some of the women prepared cedar and sage for the ceremony. When the ceremony leaders (the road chief and the fire chief) announced they were ready, we entered the lodge and walked around the fire clockwise before sitting. The fire chief burned cedar on the coals as the road chief placed a peyote button on the road. We affirmed that Mescalito was the true road chief, although Page was acting in that role for the first time. He prayed to the father, while the fire chief prayed to the mother, so we had balance.

The ceremony leaders passed medicine in the form of dried peyote and peyote tea clockwise around the circle, followed by a staff and a rattle. The person holding the staff offered either a prayer or a song while the next person rhythmically shook the rattle in sync with the drum. We continued in that pattern until we took a break at midnight. In my journal I entered the phrase: "we entered the lodge again and found that the peyote bird now had a wing and the smoking mixtures were on the left star." Today as I write this, I can't recall what I was describing at that time. We continued the ceremony until sunrise.

Harmony Hill became a resource for group meetings and

on June 15, 1977 several of us were invited there for a visit with Bhagavan Das. While waiting for him to arrive, we women sunbathed in the nude and when he arrived, he joined us in a group of about 20 people, all nude, sitting in a circle, chanting.

In August of 1977 the peyote group met at Chela's lodge again at Harmony Hill and started with a prayer smoke. In my journal, I had referred to the group as the Church of One Heart and I had prayed for the creatures of the forest who had suffered from wildfires occurring then.

A new friend, Camilla, was in contact with a man who was publicizing environmental issues that the Hopi Nation had with a mining company on their land. Together, we began raising money to bring public awareness about the issue. Camilla, Desert Sky, Lou and I sorted and stapled 400 copies of printed brochures we'd created to distribute at a public event we planned to hold at San Lorenzo Park. In October of that year we held a Hopi support group meeting in Ben Lomond. Attendees were Dennis, SkyHawk, Jim Lone Wolf and a woman named Valerie. We met at our friend Bear's house under the wing of a great horned owl.

I wrote articles for the local weekly newspaper, The Independent, about causes we supported. We also networked with a similar support group in Flagstaff.

A practicing attorney who attended our planning meetings, helped us to become a legal nonprofit group.

Lone Feather and Amber offered our group the use of their tipi for our Hopi support group meetings. On September16 ,1977 I noted in my journal that we put the lodge up after a day of scrubbing it down and a seven-year-old "owl person" found a great horned owl feather near the tipi site. We took that as a good omen.

At our first meeting in the tipi, it began to rain heavily. We got soaked because the smoke from our bonfire didn't vent well. In spite of the bad weather, we had a good meeting. The tipi was buffeted by the wind and rain, but we persevered.

Page attempted to hold a peyote circle with a new set of rules: Women wouldn't be allowed to act as fire chief any longer, menstruating women were not welcome to attend and owl medicine would be prohibited. The meeting was canceled for lack of attendance. I was surprised when Freedom asked me why no one wanted to attend Page's meeting. I lost contact with that group thereafter, but had a coincidental encounter with Freedom Lovelight (later known as Don Rose). He had become a born again Christian and was excited to share his good news but I had an urgent need to be elsewhere.

In my childhood a pair of great horned owls began calling near my bedroom and their calls evoked a strong emotion in me that often kept me awake. I felt that they were calling to me, but I was afraid to go out in the dark. My emotions ranged between fear, excitement and a sense of longing. I didn't know that the calls were owls until one day, I told my dad about hearing noises at night that kept me awake. When I described the calls to him, he identified them as "hoot" owls and assured me that they were harmless. One day he took me out on a trail and showed me an owl roosting in a tall tree. After that early childhood experience, I felt a kinship with the great feathered ones. When I hear them calling, I stop and listen. In my early childhood their calls elicited feelings of both invitation and trepidation. Now when I hear them, I feel love, admiration, gratitude and other undefinable sensations and emotions.

A woman named Angie stopped by an information table we were using on the Pacific Garden Mall mall and she decided to join our group. Her father was a medicine man and her mother was fond of coyotes (or they were fond of her). Angie had grown up on the Blackfoot Reservation. She told us that an owl was on the roof hooting while she came into the world. We bonded and she took me under her wing, taught me how to make a prayer shawl to wear and then invited me to dance with her at a powwow. Meanwhile Page was still trying to organize a peyote meeting, but walked out on a planning meeting because others refused to agree to his terms. He warned us that terrible things would happen to other participants unless his rules were adopted. I was no longer interested in his group at that point.

In December 1977 we planned a four day fundraiser for the purpose of renting a hall. AIM (American Indian Movement) member, Bill Wahpepah called and suggested we make ourselves known to his community. Bill, was developing an after school program for native children in Oakland. He said he'd heard about us and added, "Not that I'm doubting your credibility, but we've had some opportunists." I explained that we were a newly formed group and were working with the Intertribal Student Alliance at Cabrillo College. He mentioned that Russell Means' brother was in town and was looking for a place to speak and that they would attend our event in February.

I have a newspaper clipping with the following information: "American Indian Benefit: The Santa Cruz Native American Support Group is hosting a bash at the Good Fruit Company to raise money and consciousness for a number of causes. David Tate and friends, Climbing Sun, the Solar Minstrels and Freedom Lovelight will all perform and T. Michael Walker will speak."

Subsequently, Bill invited us to attend a fundraiser in Oakland. He came to Santa Cruz and drove a group of us to the Peoples Temple where we were greeted by Jim Jones. They had a large gathering and lots of food and I don't know how money was raised, but Bill spent some time talking to Jones while the rest of us sat around and ate food. Perhaps Jones donated money to Bill's after school project. I had no idea we had been guests of a cult leader until later.

In January of 1978 Angie, Debra, Bobby Lee Shippen and I went to Oakland for Bill Wahpepah's Survival School's open house. Will Knapp played his guitar, Bill said a prayer and asked that we all be good Indian people, then added, "If you're ever in trouble, come here."

In February we had a gathering at the Veterans Hall in Santa Cruz. Attendees included Climbing Sun, Pat Orozco, Yvonne Wanrow and Floyd Westerman.

In March Dennis Banks and Angie held a press conference at Cabrillo College. The next day we presented a Native American Women's panel. Although I don't recall that event I do have a news clipping about it.

In 1980, I transferred to UCSC and chose to major in Community Studies, an interdisciplinary study consisting of political science and sociology. In addition to classes in those subjects, I was required to perform a field study. I had been voted president of the Santa Cruz Indian Council and I worked with other council members to obtain a grant from the Hewlett-Packard Foundation. The grant helped us purchase Native American cultural materials for use in local elementary schools. Al Dixon, a member of the Indian Council, also served as an administrator of the Santa Cruz County Board of Education. He was instrumental in helping us acquire and donate the cultural materials.

During my tenure as president of the group, we obtained permission from authorities at UCSC and implemented an annual intertribal powwow to be held on school grounds. I'm unsure when those annual powwows ended, but I believe they continued into the early 1990s.

In the early 1980s an Oglala Sioux medicine man called

"Stampede" moved from the Pine Ridge Reservation to Santa Cruz to attend Cabrillo College. He performed a ceremony at T. Mike Walker's tipi at Cabrillo on April 30, 1980. When I arrived there, he was preparing by circling the tipi and blowing on his flute which had been constructed from an eagle bone. Inside the tipi he began the ceremony by singing a song to invite the spirits. Stampede blessed Mike's pipe and stated that the pipe belongs to the animals and that elk is Mike's medicine.

Stampede also talked about his vision quests and stated that he had been adopted by the "owl people". He ended his prayer with an owl call.

Tribal beliefs vary regarding the role of various animals. Many with heritage in the plains honor owls, but some (particularly in the southwest) feel that owls have a negative quality. This helps to explain the disagreements some of us had with Page's rules regarding prohibiting owl energy in peyote meetings.

Grandfather Semu of the Chumash tribe moved his camp from a canyon near Los Angeles to the Santa Margarita area. I first met him and his group while I was living in Los Angeles. I was happy to spend time with him when he visited Santa Cruz in the early 1980s. I admired his wisdom and I loved his sense of humor.

When he visited Santa Cruz, I reminded Grandfather that I had first met him when he was camped near Los Angeles and he responded, "The year was 1972. That was really fun." He said that the authorities had tried to give him a citation for having a fire in a tent, but he was able to avoid it by explaining that his "tent" was a tipi.

After obtaining a BA degree at UCSC, I earned a Masters degree in Library Science with a focus on technology at San Jose State University and I accepted a position in Los Angeles where I managed the conversion of a library's old card catalog to an automated online system. After that project was completed, I was recruited by Carlyle Systems, a technology company, headquartered in Emeryville. They developed software for university libraries. I moved to Oakland and visited Santa Cruz frequently but I missed living there.

In the early 1990s, a start-up software consulting company, Thuridion, in Scotts Valley, hired me to manage their in-house resource library. I returned to Santa Cruz, married Santa Cruz native, Rob Watson, and plan to spend the rest of my life here.

It's great to be home again.

————————————

Sadly, Russell Means, Bill Wahpepah, Lee Brightman, Dennis Banks and Stampede aka Wilmer Mesteth have all passed from this life. They left an honorable legacy.

Hounded: Huey P. Newton in Santa Cruz: 1973-74, 1977-80
by Willard Charles Ford (May 24,1991)

Thanks to Mom, Paul and Matthew.

Preface

I first came to the University of California at Santa Cruz in the Fall of 1987. The summer before, UCSC informed me through the mail that I was entering a "free market of ideas." That same summer, my uncle, Paul Lee, sent me a UCSC t-shirt, printed with the school motto, "Making the Ideal Real." A letter from UCSC described the institution as an alternative to other large, public universities in that undergraduate teaching was stressed. That all sounded good to me, so I packed my car and drove from Los Angeles to Santa Cruz where my loving relatives were waiting to feed, clothe, house, and teach me how to do the college thing.

When I was selecting my first series of courses, I came across a class on "revolutionary literature." I was very interested and attended the first lecture. I was surprised by the syllabus for the class which included, among other things, Karl Marx's *Communist Manifesto* and Franz Fanon's *The Wretched of the Earth* I enrolled in the course.

For the required research paper I decided to do a biography of Huey P. Newton, the co-founder of the Black Panther Party in Oakland, and a graduate of UCSC, where Dr. Newton had earned a B.A.(1973-74) and a Ph.D. (1977-80). I knew I had an excellent source of information in my uncle, Paul Lee, who had been Newton's faculty advisor at UCSC. Paul related his experiences with Newton, whom he believed to be a man of great historical importance. I was excited and eager to begin.

Huey Newton Sunday received doctorate degree from Chancellor Robert Sinsheimer.

Huey Newton Gets Doctorate Degree

Black Panther co-founder Huey P. Newton, a revolutionary of the 1960s, received a doctorate degree from UCSC Sunday.

UCSC Chancellor Robert Sinsheimer presented Newton with the degree in the history of consciousness, an interdisciplinary program on the history of social philosophy.

Newton, 38, received his diploma after three years. He earned a bachelor's degree in education from UCSC in 1974.

Anthropologist Trinh Pandey, one of Newton's advisors on his doctoral thesis, "War Against the Panthers: A Study of Repression in America," praised Newton.

"We really did not know what to expect, but on the whole I think Newton has done rather well," Pandey said.

Pandey called Newton's thesis "a very good job. He really has a very good mind."

Newton, who lived in Oakland while he was writing his thesis, kept a low profile on campus.

The former revolutionary was charged with attempted murder after a shooting at a Seaside bar in 1978, but the matter was dismissed before going to trial.

Newton, who has been a defendant in seven felony trials, five at them, in murder counts, long claimed that government officials conspired to defame him and to destroy the Black Panthers.

The late FBI Director, J. Edgar Hoover, once called the Panthers the most dangerous group in the United States.

The Panther leader spent 22 months in prison after being found guilty of the 1967 murder of an Oakland policeman. An appellate court later reversed the decision, and the murder charge was dropped.

In 1974, Newton was accused of fatally shooting a 17-year-old prostitute on a street corner, and of pistol-whipping his tailor at Newton's plush, lakeside penthouse apartment.

Newton jumped $42,000 bail and fled to Cuba, voluntarily returning three years later. The murder charge was dropped after two juries failed to reach a verdict.

He was acquitted of the assault charge.

Today, Newton barely resembles the gun-rattling revolutionary who harangued crowds a decade ago.

"The most dangerous groups to the people of the world are the Pentagon, the CIA, the U.S. military, the local police, the avaricious businessmen and the lying politicians...all are guilty of crimes against the people and the verdict is death," Newton said 15 years ago.

But the Panthers apparently have toned down their past, sometimes violent, behavior.

"We're just not looking at the Panthers anymore," said an intelligence officer with the Oakland police.

As a naive freshman, I thought the professor would be impressed by my choice, because the ideology of the Black Panther Party is a revolutionary ideology that relies on the thoughts and words of both Marx and Fanon. When I approached the professor to tell him about my plan, he said he would not read a paper on Newton or the Black Panther Party, because, he did not respect Dr. Newton.

I was intimidated by the professor's response to my chosen topic, and surprised by the his resentment and hostility towards the man I had been told was a hero. I could not understand why the subject of Newton was so incendiary and intolerable. Afraid to enrage the professor further, I wrote an uninspired history of the Chinese Cultural Revolution in relation to another book on the syllabus.

It took two years to recover from this incident. Not once in that time did I approach a teacher after class or at his/her office hours. The rejection of the teacher silenced me.

What facilitated my recovery were two events; the announcement of the death of Dr. Newton, and a professor who was supportive in my decision to make Newton the focus of my academic career.

When Newton was murdered, numerous articles describing Newton as a gangster, a bully, an intellectual midget, a thief, and a killer, appeared in newspapers and magazines throughout the nation. But what grabbed my attention most was an article in the *Santa Cruz Sentinel* in which a professor at UCSC described Newton's academic achievements as undistinguished; directly contradictory to what my uncle had told me. What was particularly alarming about the professor's comments were that they laid siege to Newton's character via his academic work.

I explained my interest in Newton to Dr. Marilyn Patton, a professor of American Studies. When I told her about the professors' reaction to Newton and the media assault on his character, she urged me to write a paper about him. So I began to wade through Newton's work, as well as articles about his death, and interview people who had worked with him at UCSC. She encouraged me to immerse myself in the subject and was very helpful in sifting through the material. At the end of the quarter, I presented her with a paper on the media's vilification of Huey P. Newton. This undergraduate thesis is an outgrowth of that paper.

Contrary to the opinion of that first professor, Newton is worthy of our attention. This thesis is my attempt to fulfill the promise of the university as a "free market of ideas," and expose the closed minded world of academic fundamentalism where value judgments dictate subject matter in an arbitrary and willful way.

William James once wrote that, "We ought ... delicately and profoundly to respect one another's mental freedom; then only shall we bring about the intellectual republic; then only shall we have the spirit of inner tolerance ... then only shall we live and let live, in speculative as well as practical things" (Smith, *Killing the Spirit.*, p. 103-104).

Methodology

I relied heavily on interviews with professors who had taught Huey P. Newton at UCSC, as well as others who knew him there, to reconstruct his time in Santa Cruz (1973-74, 1977-80). Among those interviewed on tape were Paul Lee, Newton's academic advisor, Page Smith, another advisor, who served on Newton's thesis review committee, William Moore, former "Sergeant of Arms" of the Black Panther Party, Robert Trivers, professor of biology, Johnny Chesko, the bodyguard of Newton, who drove the "escape boat" to Cuba when Huey

fled the country, and Hayden White, Chairman of the History
of Consciousness Program. Untaped interviews included Bert
Schneider, a financial contributor to the Black Panther Party,
and executor to Newton's estate, Billie Harris, the secretary of
the History of Consciousness Board, who knew Newton, as
well as Noel King, professor of religion. Informal discussions
with Ralph Abraham, professor of mathematics, and Burney
LeBoeuf, professor of biology, helped fill out some of the
rough edges.

Other taped material included a talk and lecture given by
Bobby Seale for the Second Annual Huey P. Newton Memorial
Lecture, a round table discussion with Madalyn Rucker, a
member of the Party, and David Hilliard, who served as the
Chairman of the Black Panther Party, when both Newton and
Seale were in jail.

When I first started gathering facts about Newton's time in
Santa Cruz, interviews were essential in the reconstruction of
events. Only in the past week was I able to acquire Newton's
academic records, which have helped in organizing the
sequence of events that made up his academic career.

Primary Materials/ Outline

This thesis documents Huey P. Newton's undergraduate
and graduate education at the University of California, Santa
Cruz. Aside from numerous newspaper articles, alarmingly
unreliable, very little has been written about this period of
Newton's life, and I know of no source that documents his
education in Santa Cruz, or for that matter, his academic work
at all.

For historical background on Newton and the Black
Panther Party, I have relied on Newton's autobiography,
Revolutionary Suicide, his doctoral dissertation, *War Against*

the Panthers: A Study of Repression in America, and Bobby
Seale's two autobiographies, *A Lonely Rage* and *Seize the Time*.
For a review of the federal government war on the Black
Panther Party, I used Churchill and Vander Wall's *Agents of
Repression*, as well as Newton's dissertation. In order to dissect
his political ideology, which was closely related to his work
at UCSC, I read Newton's *To Die For the People*, Paul Tillich's
Systematic Theology to develop the Son of Man theme, as well
as Newton's collaborative book with Erik Erikson, *In Search of
Common Ground*. For an historical background of UCSC and
a critique of the university as an institution I relied heavily on
Page Smith's *Killing the Spirit*, as well as various articles from
the *City on a Hill Press* and the *Santa Cruz Sentinel*.

To fill out the picture, various books, periodicals, official
school documents and interviews were used.

The Introduction of this work is a review of the early
history of the Black Panther Party, for the most part before
Newton's arrival at UCSC. Chapter One is a summary history
of race relations at UCSC, focusing on the proposal for an
African American Studies college to be named in honor
of Malcolm X. Chapter Two is Newton's history at UCSC,
focusing on three main subject matters: religion, biology,
and social science, as well as a description of his thesis work.
Chapter Three deals with the faculty's reaction to Newton. It
is a simple analysis of the conflict, focusing on the negative
impressions of some faculty and the counter-statements of
those who supported him. Chapter Four explains how the
institution is not designed to deal with marginal people, which
includes Newton. Chapter Five discusses the antagonisms
between Newton and campus Marxist academics. Chapter
Six chronicles Newton's arrest in Santa Cruz which confirmed
fears that Newton was dangerous and somehow unworthy
of a university degree. It is a media analysis using only the

Santa Cruz Sentinel and interviews. The Conclusion outlines Newton's studies and how they help us understand him, paying special attention to the critical themes of his work.

Introduction

In 1966, Huey Percy Newton and Bobby Seale founded the Black Panther Party for Self-Defense (BPP) in Oakland, California. From day one, the Party defined itself as a revolutionary political organization. Newton, the chief ideologist of the Party, developed a Marxist-Leninist derived ideology of "revolutionary intercommunalism,"[1] which was used to interpret socioeconomic, historical and political phenomenon and as a framework for a general improvement in the quality of life for African Americans.

Tired of "armchair" revolutionaries whom Newton believed contributed very little to the betterment of the material conditions of people of color and the poor, most notably cultural nationalists, like Ron Kerenga's *United Slaves* (US) and the *American Communist Party*, the BPP went to work. As the self-proclaimed inheritors of the teachings of El Hajj Malik El Shabazz (Malcolm X), the Panthers concentrated their efforts on putting theory into practice. With the goal of lifting the consciousness of all people by unveiling to them the socio-political powers that were oppressing them, Newton hoped to lead the people in their first steps toward their own emancipation.

In its first stage of development, the BPP was· a citizen protection group formed in reaction to increasing police brutality against blacks in the Oakland ghetto:[2] later the BPP's "police patrols" became secondary to a more expansive effort to battle the plight of poor blacks and other unemployables (the "lumpen-proletariat") confined to the poverty and crime

stricken area of East Oakland. Later in the development of the
Party, coalitions with other political entities such as the *Peace
and Freedom Party*, the *American Indian Movement* and the
Young Patriots, resulted in widespread political influence for
the BPP. Slowly but surely, BPP chapters popped up across the
country and around the globe as the BPP became a world-
wide political force.

What differentiated the BPP from earlier civil rights
organizations was that they conscientiously recruited from
the traditional unemployable masses off "the block," and not
the educated middle-classes. Newton grew up on the streets
of Oakland and had a firm belief in the potential for social
change that lay manifest in the masses of the underclass.

The BPP organized predominantly young men and women
of equal numbers to implement their Ten-Point Program. The
Program stated their basic demands:

1. We want freedom. We want power to determine the
    destiny of our black community.
2. We want full employment of our people.
3. We want an end to the robbery by the capitalists of our
    black community.
4. We want decent housing fit for shelter of human beings.
5. We want education for our people that exposes the true
    nature of this decadent American society. We want
    education that teaches us our true history and our role
    in present-day society.
6. We want all black men to be exempt from military
    service.
7. We want an immediate end to police brutality and
    murder of black people.
8. We want freedom for all black men held in federal, state,
    county, and city prisons and jails.

9. We want all black people when brought to trial to be tried in court by a jury of their peer group or people from their black communities as defined by the Constitution of the United States.
10. We want land, bread, housing, education, clothing, justice, and peace (Newton, *War Against the Panthers*, p.141-144).

As a community based organization, the first role the BPP for Self-Defense played in Oakland was to follow the police and observe them in the course of their "duties." Armed with guns, and more significantly, law books, the BPP for Self-Defense took to the streets to *police the police*. Standing at a legally determined "reasonable distance," the Panthers observed the police and informed a detainee or arrestee of his/her constitutional rights. They were aware of the law through Newton's legal studies and made certain never to break it. The patrols were successful in that they sent the police running from their communities.

The images provoked by armed black men and women in the minds of racists when confronted by armed resistance to oppression led them to be characterized by representatives of the power structure as aggressively violent and even anti-white. The very idea of blacks patrolling the police in their communities, or the idea of blacks with guns, were ideas offensive to the "moral majority's" notion of social order. In *In Search for Common Ground*, a collaboration between Newton and Erik Erikson, the latter wrote:

> "...those who created the law certainly did not envisage anybody but white men doing so, nor did they envisage anybody but potential lawbreakers as the ones to be patrolled by vigilant citizens in an

ill defined and frontier territory...The west is still
frontier territory and the lawless are often those in
control of the law. Police break the law under the
pretense of protecting the law. Newton, by inspir-
ing the armed patrols, made the 'law enforcers' into
the 'symbol' of uniformed and armed 'lawlessness.
Newton does this by turning the imagery of policing against the police by assuming the righteous
role of enforcing the law. Using the book and the
gun Newton used traditional symbolism that has
been used by Germans and Zionists alike. To give
the blacks and pigs transvalued images is to take
great risks, as it provokes the law and enrages them,
leading to the possibility of violent backlash (Fred
Hampton). Newton gives a positive identity to a
negative one; the retreating Black Panther striking
out in self-defense (p.45-47)."

The Panthers were vastly different than any popularly
accepted organization before them (SNCC, SCLC, NAACP,
CORE, Nation of Islam, etc.). The BPP for Self-Defense,
in their initial phases, did not support electoral politics or
non-violence as the proper techniques to combat what they
characterized as their "colonized" condition. Erikson rather
poignantly represented Newton's belief that armed discipline,
and the following violence, are necessary prerequisites to
non-violent solutions, by putting the use of nonviolence in its
proper historical perspective. He wrote that,

> ... there is a relationship between violence and
> non-violence which is rarely considered by those
> who have not studied the question. Gandhi, in fact,
> is often derided for having believed from time to

time in the necessity for his nation to learn universal armed expertise before they could truly de-
nounce the use of arms... nonviolence does not just
mean abstention from violence which one would
not have the means to carry through anyway, but
the renunciation of armed tactics one would well
know how to use (p.49).

Indeed, Huey Newton, quoting Mao, believed that "political
power grows out of the barrel of a gun." In this he stressed the
word "grows" which was an attempt to say the gun was not
an end in itself, but merely a tool or a means of achieving the
end (Erikson, Newton, p.64). In other words, the Panthers
picked up the gun in order to get rid of it, whereas the power
structure, represented by its various policing forces, use the
gun to maintain control (p.115).

Having lost faith in the ideal of nonviolent resistance, the
Panthers picked up the gun. However, in so doing, the BPP
did not support violence as the ultimate problem solver,
but rather were working towards a time when non-violent
resistance techniques would be relevant. Newton believed that
asking black people to accept nonviolence as the only proper
tool for liberation was "... insane because you are asking a
people who suffer materially for an ideal that will not benefit
them" (Erikson, Newton, p.63). In other words, he saw the
violence of the power structure in a completely different moral
light than the nonviolent self-defense of the oppressed in the
tradition of Martin Luther King, Jr. and Gandhi.

The world was made aware of the BPP when a fully
armed contingent of Panthers, led by Bobby Seale, entered
the State Capitol building in Sacramento on May 2, 1967 to
demonstrate their dissatisfaction with the impending Mulford
Act.[3] Prior to the armed patrols that were conducted by the

BPP in their communities, the gun control lobby had found little support in state government. Having become aware of the BPP for Self-Defense, the power structure moved to curb their growing power and influence by banning the right of all Americans to carry guns. In effect, the California legislature moved to "reinterpret" the Second Amendment of the Constitution which plainly decrees that all U.S. citizens have the right to bear arms and that no police or militia force can infringe upon that right. The passing of the Mulford Act signaled an end to a chapter in the history of the BPP for Self Defense: they no longer could conduct armed patrols of their communities.

In order to deemphasize the symbolic role of the gun, the Black Panther Party for Self-Defense dropped "Self-Defense" to become the Black Panther Party. In a similar move, Huey Newton changed his title from the 'Minister of Defense" to "Servant of the People" (Newton. *To Die For The People.*, p. xvii). No longer able to count on the imagery of the gun to attract attention to themselves, the real heart of the Party, the community programs, served to draw new people into the Party. But this move away from the rhetoric of the gun was not a step backward as many radicals suggested, most notably Ron Kerenga. In *To Die for the People* Newton rejects the idea that the BPP is reformist, because he states that revolution is a process (p.47). In *In Search of Common Ground* he states that revolution is a "...contradiction between the old and the new in the process of development. Anything can be revolutionary at a particular point in time" (p.101).

Huey Newton, the Party's primary field general and theorist, was instrumental in the implementation of these "survival programs" aimed at alleviating the immediate hardships of ghetto life. While the survival programs were always the most important aspect of the Party, they had never received the attention of the popular press. Included among these programs were transportation for the elderly and the families of political prisoners, free heath care, including sickle-cell anemia testing, free education at fully accredited schools sensitive to black cultural values, and free breakfast for school children (Newton, *War Against the Panthers*, p.43). All of these programs were successful in the black community where they served thousands of needy individuals ignored by social welfare. To fund the survival programs, the BPP called for widespread community support. If such support was not forthcoming, the BPP was not against boycotting stores in their communities, causing the press to call them "extortionists."

Reacting to the "communistic" flavor of these programs, the law "enforcement" agencies of this nation, under the guidance of J. Edgar Hoover's FBI, worked to dismantle the Black Panther Party. Hoover announced that he considered the BPP, "the greatest threat to the internal security of the country" (*Agents of Repression*, p.77). Noam Chomsky commented on the government conspiracy to destroy the BPP in his introduction he wrote for Nelson Blackstock's *COINTELPRO* referring at the same time to the extraordinary popularity of the Party,

> A top secret Special Report for the president in June 1970 gives some insight into the motivation for the actions undertaken by the government to destroy the Black Panther Party. The report describes the party as "the most active and dangerous black extremist group in the United States." Its "hard core members" were estimated at 800, but "a recent poll indicates that approximately 25 per cent of the black population has great respect for the

BPP, including 43 per cent of blacks under 21 years of age." On the basis of such estimates of the potential of the party, the repressive apparatus of the state proceeded against it to ensure that it did not succeed in organizing as a substantial social or political force. We may add that in this case, government repression proved quite successful."

What separates the explicit destruction of the BPP from many other conspiracy theories is that information concerning this is derived from government sources, via the Freedom of Information Act. In files acquired by Newton, Hoover called upon the FBI and all of their affiliates to "exploit all avenues of creating ... dissension within the ranks of the BPP." The director of the FBI called for, "... recipient offices ... to submit imaginative and hard-hitting counterintelligence measures aimed at crippling the BPP'" (Churchill, Vander Wall, *Agents of Repression*. p. 64).

FBI methods used to destroy the BPP were many and far reaching. "(H)ard-hitting counterintelligence measures" included anything that would destroy the Party, both internally and externally:

1. Bogus mail attributed to Party members was sent to other Party members with the aim of creating artificial splits between Party members. The most notable of these splits was between Eldridge Cleaver, then Minister of Information, and Huey P. Newton, both of whom were in political exile from the United States at the time.
2. Fake propaganda was distributed throughout the black and white communities aimed at misrepresenting the BPP to the public. At one point a fake coloring book, bearing the logo of the BPP, that contained racist

remarks was distributed by the FBI to supporters of the Party. This resulted in the withdrawal of funds by more conservative supporters of the Party.

3. Harassment arrests designed to tie up and drain funds, as well as confirm false media representations of the Panthers as aggressively violent and racist, were common. Bobby Seale was arrested immediately following a fund-raiser for the Free Huey fund in which the BPP collected $10,000 for Newton's legal defense. Seale's bail was set at $7,000.

4. The "bad-jacketing" of legitimate members by leading other members to believe that they were agents. Stokely Carmichael was a victim of this tactic. He was badjacketed by the FBI as a CIA agent and subsequently dismissed by Newton from the BPP.

5. The fabrication of evidence to be used in illegitimate cases against members of the Party, especially Newton and Seale. Newton was involved in at least two COINTELPRO generated court trials a year. While working with the Party, he was never once convicted of a felony. Likewise, Seale was jailed numerous times on trumped up charges, most notably when he was charged with inciting a riot at the Democratic National Convention. The case was the infamous "Chicago 8" trial (although later it became "Chicago 7" due to Seale receiving a separate trial).

6. Political assassinations of members of the BPP. Among those killed in covert inter-departmental efforts to destroy the BPP were Alprentice "Bunchy" Carter and John Huggins in Los Angeles and Fred Hampton[4] in Chicago, as well as many others.

7. Placing of infiltrators within the Party to act as provocateurs to help in creating an image of Panther

aggression. These agents also provided information for the FBI, as was the case when William O'Neal supplied floor plans for the infamous raid by Chicago Police on Fred Hampton's apartment.

As can be seen by the viciousness of this COINTELPRO operation, Hoover would not rest until his operatives had destroyed the BPP. Hoover saw the eradication of the BPP survival programs as a vital step in the dismantling of the BPP. By destroying these programs he hoped to diminish the positive public image that the Party earned with these programs that served poor blacks who increasingly turned out to receive aid that was conspicuously absent from government services (Churchill, Vander Wall, p.63). The free breakfast program in particular was perceived by Hoover as the most dangerous political program of the BPP, perhaps because it was so well received by the communities that it served, as well as by the media which reported its success. At the Second Annual Huey P. Newton Memorial lecture, Bobby Seale said that in an attempt to downplay the significance of this program, the Oakland Police Department, out of embarrassment more than anything else, started their own breakfast program, to pull attention away from the BPP. One year later, after having diluted propogandistic importance of the Panther program, the Oakland Police breakfast program was silently discontinued. According to one confidant, Huey Newton was pleased at the irony that such a "benign" program was interpreted to be such a threat.

Newton explained the reason for the FBI's violent resistance to an organization like the BPP in *War Against the Panthers*. "To the BPP, government opposition to its existence was expected as partial confirmation of its *raison d'etre* ... 'Revolutionary intercommunalism' ... served to pit the BPP and the government law enforcement against each other in ideological struggle" (p.34). The basic contradiction of interests is maintained by the status quo, because capitalists have a vested interest in maintaining the "natural order" of things (p.5).

Considering the extent to which the federal government went to dismantle the BPP, many people wonder how such a small and relatively powerless political force could survive. Newton explains in *In Search of Common Ground* that the ideology of the BPP allowed it to cope with external and internal contradictions, even emphasized the inherent usefulness of contradiction in developing a sophisticated ideological framework with which to explain phenomenon. Revolutionary intercommunalism, which relies heavily on dialectical materialism,

> ... gave the Party a perhaps unexpected asset in its struggle for survival ... to the BPP leadership, its ideology, despite the sound of dogma it may have conveyed to others, served it as a pragmatic methodology for interpreting events. A central tenet of revolutionary intercommunalism, for example, is that "contradiction is the ruling principal of the universe," that everything is in a constant state of transformation. Recognition of these principals gave Party leaders an ability to grow through a self-criticism that many other political organizations seemed to lack (p.35).

Such a dialectical understanding of political maturation allowed the BPP to survive its development from a black nationalist group to a black internationalist group and finally to a global intercommunalist organization that recognized the universal nature of mankind.

Perhaps even stranger that the mindless characterization of the BPP as aggressively "violent" was the media representation of the BPP as a racist organization. The BPP in no way endorsed feelings of racial superiority. Newton wrote that, "... the BPP is not based on hate. We feel that our revolutionary program must be guided by love-armed love as we sometimes call it" (Erikson. Newton, p.62), because armed love leads to mutual respect and dignity and only out of equality can two people really love one another (Erikson, Newton, p.79). The BPP spread the idea that unless a common identity is sought and found there will be no solution to world problems as they are.

Newton believed this universal identity would help counter the effects of forces bent on making black people feel a depreciated sense of self-worth (Erikson, Newton, p.38). Furthermore, Newton believed the dialectical basis of the ideology of the Party would lead to the end of racism and ethnocentrism. By controlling all material resources, including the media, the tools to destroy racism and ethnocentrism will be in the hands of the people, because they will be in control of "... their own subconscious attitudes ... and for the first time in history they will have a more rather than a less conscious relationship to the material world" (Erikson, Newton, p.41). Erikson clarifies this idea in his statement about media control of imagery and how it helps form individual and/or group identity,

> ... we are a part of a largely unconscious con-
> spiracy of maintaining a collective image of reality
> composed pretty much in equal measure of clear
> facts, debatable opinions, and outright delusions.
> And so, as I have pointed out, does the exploited

class or race accept a "reality" daily enforced by the
media serving those in power,-which is exactly why
revolutions have to be shocking in order to really
unhinge existing identities (p.52).

While Newton was belittled by the popular press and
ridiculed by many in this country as a violent and racist
fanatic, his international reputation as a Marxist scholar and
leader of international black liberation tells of an individual
of great historical importance. Paul Lee, Newton's faculty
advisor at UCSC, said Newton was considered the chief living
symbolic leader of Afro American liberation thought. As if
to confirm this estimation, Newton was invited to China by
Mao Tse-tung (before President Richard Nixon) as a symbolic
move to support the BPP. Upon arrival in China, Newton and
his entourage were given a state welcome by Chou Enlai and
treated as representatives of a socialist movement of great
significance. Lee believes this gesture, on Mao's part, verified
Newton's international significance as an individual in the
vanguard of implementing revolutionary movements world-
wide.

Huey Newton carried the baton of Afro American
liberation in a direct historical line from Martin Luther
King, Jr. and Malcolm X, completing a three step process
which caused America and the world to reconsider the "race
question."

It seems that Newton and the BPP were a natural
development in the ideological, philosophical and religious
transformation of the movement for black liberation. It is
important to view this transformation, in that it illustrates the
reasons for the approach to social change that was taken by
the BPP.

First, there was Martin Luther King Jr. who utilized

nonviolent resistance tactics. He envisioned one humanity where the "lion will lay down with the lamb." With the umbrella of Christianity, he acted as the symbolic leader of the more conservative civil rights movement. But black people were still being killed, including King himself, leading many to be disillusioned with the potential for nonviolence to achieve liberation.

Then came Malcolm X, who represented the logical alternative. Violence in self-defense gained wide acceptance in many black communities, especially among the young, as the only realistic way to combat white aggression. To society at large, Malcolm X and those he represented were putting out a message that liberation was to be achieved "by any means necessary." His support for the Nation of Islam (Elijah Muhammad), and the religious contention that whites were the devil, frightened the predominantly white and Christian, power holding elite. Later in his life, he embraced the more traditional Muslim vision of one humanity and worked for concrete progress in race relations and social change. Regardless, many blacks were continually brutalized and Malcolm X was the next to fall as an assassinated leader.

With the "failure" of the previous two steps comes Huey P. Newton. The BPP replaces the world identity of Islam with the coalition politics of revolutionary intercommunalism. Symbol and image play an important part in how Newton and the BPP were perceived by others. As seen in a famous photo, Newton was the physical embodiment of resistance to white oppression. Wearing his BPP uniform, with one hand on a rifle and the other on a Zulu spear (although some suggest that it is a harpoon for going after Melville's Moby Dick, the great white whale) he exemplifies the right to self-defense (Seale. *Seize the Time*, p.222). Like Malcolm X, the BPP demanded equal treatment "or else." The difference lay in the fact that Malcolm X threatened to get guns and defend himself. The BPP were armed and waiting, thus putting into practice the teachings of Malcolm X. The picture of Newton is the personification of white America's worst fears; a black, suicidal,[5] communist-armed to the teeth.

This symbolic resistance became real with the "storming" of the State Capitol. The photographs that came out of this nonviolent demonstration were a catalyst for sparking horror in the collective imagination of most white Americans. Ignoring the political and symbolic significance of the Panther's actions, the press portrayed the plea for the restoration of African American citizens' constitutional rights as proof of the Panthers insurrectionary aims (Newton, *War Against the Panthers*, p.40-41).

Chapter One:
Preparing for Huey — the History of Race Relations at UCSC.

In the Spring Quarter of 1973, Huey P. Newton entered the University of California at Santa Cruz, to pursue a course of study in philosophy and social science (Appendix 1). In order to understand the diverse faculty reactions that Huey Newton encountered in Santa Cruz, it is important to set the political-historical tone of the campus at the time of his arrival.

The negative reactions that Huey Newton encountered at UCSC were described by William Moore, the Santa Cruz spokesman for the Black Liberation Movement, in an interview, as "matters of race." Moore said the resistance to Newton can be linked to the series of events that make up the history of the university's relationship with people of color.

When Moore first came to Santa Cruz in 1967, UCSC was a fledgling university, composed primarily of white,

conservative, middle-class people who were separated from
the political turmoil that had overcome the big university
campuses. Armed with the slogan, "Making the Ideal Real,"
UCSC was proposed as a model for the alternative, public
university, with emphasis placed on increased student/
teacher contact, small colleges (twenty were planned), non-
competitive scholastics and sensitivity to the needs of all
students (*Campus Handbook*, 1987). The motto of Cowell
College, the first to open, was "the pursuit of truth in the
company of friends." As such, the university was founded on
the utopian principles of the earliest Christian "settlers" of
this continent, who came in an attempt to create a "City on a
Hill," free from religious persecution. The school newspaper is
called "City on a Hill."

But like the earliest settlements, the ideals were somehow
abandoned in favor of burning witches. A witch was an
individual who didn't conform to the system. Like most
bureaucratic institutions, UCSC had lost its vision and had
become a miniature of the world, reflecting the deficiencies
of society, ignoring it's goal as a project for social renovation.
It was this decaying ideal that William Moore encountered in
'67.

In 1967, Moore was prompted by his boss at the Sylvania
light bulb company to "get involved." He soon became the
leading spokesman of the Black Liberation Movement (BLM)
in Santa Cruz, giving provocative and incendiary speeches
in the revolutionary tradition of El Hajj Malik El Shabazz
(Malcolm X). By the summer of '68, the same summer as
the Chicago Police Riots during the Democratic National
Convention, Moore had embarked on a political mission in
the most volatile summer of the decade.

William Moore represented a call from the black
community of Santa Cruz to name the yet to be built College

Seven, "Malcolm X College." With this overt move to alter the dominant conception of an "alternative" university to incorporate the needs of African Americans, Moore believed the attitudes of those in power at UCSC were revealed. Moore said that at this point in time, "If you were a black person at Santa Cruz and you created a problem, they'd just fire you."

Tensions between African American students and a conservative run UCSC bureaucracy were inflamed when, in March, 1968, when the campus organization "Students for Huey," invited Bobby Seale and Eldridge Cleaver to speak at a rally in support of Huey Newton, then jailed for voluntary manslaughter in the shooting death of Oakland police officer John Frey (the conviction was later reversed). While Seale was allowed to come, the administration barred Cleaver from speaking by virtue of an obscure, never before invoked, UC policy that did not permit convicted felons to speak on campus (*City on a Hill*, "Poor Students for Huey").

A few months later, in a statement dated August 18, 1968, the BLM demanded College Seven be named in honor of Malcolm X, focusing on "The Black Experience." The BLM proposal demanded that teachers be from The Black Experience, that a room be set aside for discussing The Black Experience, and that this college be designed by an architect of The Black Experience (Appendix 2). William Moore, the chief spokesman of the BLM, announced that the college would not discriminate against any group, but would simply be involved in the study of The Black Experience, an experience in which all races have a stake.

Moore said that by accepting the proposal, the university would be moving towards important symbolic changes that would help race relations by making good on white America's promise of self-improvement for African Americans through education.

For many radicals, liberals, and people of color, the proposed college signaled the realization of promised dreams of equality in education, as well as a return to the egalitarian ideals of the university. For many moderates, a Malcolm X College exposed their political neutrality; they didn't know who to believe or what to do. For conservatives, the proposed project was seen as an attack on the established order.

Anticipating resistance to the idea, Moore presented the college as a sensible alternative to the violence that had claimed the lives of whites and African Americans alike, promising that it would be a "'non-violent thing ...There's no reason not to support it.'" (*Sentinel*, "Black college idea given circulation!" 8/22/68).

Moore particularly stressed the importance of associating the name of Malcolm X with the college, stating that "'we as black people have picked this man's name. To black people this man symbolizes the black experience and this is what the school is all about.'" Moore vehemently denied charges that Malcolm X himself was a racist, citing his later rejection of the Nation of Islam in favor of the more universal Muslim tradition, and denied that the hiring policies of a college that recruited from The Black Experience would be an indication of reverse racism ("Black college idea given circulation," 8/22/68). Moore made this clear in our interview when he asked, "If we had black students in white universities why couldn't we have whites in black colleges?... If colleges can be named after white heroes, why can't we name colleges after black heroes?."

Within ten days of issuing the demands, Moore was called to speak before the county supervisors. Their reaction to Moore's proposal indicated stressed race relations between members of the local power structure and people of color. Upon hearing his proposal, Moore was ridiculed by many of the supervisors. Tom Black, without much thought, compared the call for a College of Malcolm X to the establishment of "'...a Brendan Behan college for all those Irish derelicts.'" Likewise, Robert Burton mocked the BLM demand by slighting both Native Americans and black Americans with the comment, "We should have some teepees up there.'" Yet another supervisor, Vincent Locatelli, captured the general flavor of the response to Moore when he indicated violence by stating, "'bring 'em down. I'll tell them what I think of them'" (*Sentinel* "Supervisors Ask Spokesman To Explain Malcolm X College," 8/28/68).

Other conservative community members came out to bash the proposed college for black studies. Mrs. H. R. Lans, a local representative of conservatism, stated that she would not support such a move back to what she labeled as "segregation." An Estonian, she considered herself a member of a minority group, and with ignorance and arrogance stated that she would never "'ask to establish an all-Estonian college.'" Her general response to the supporters of the Malcolm X College was, "'If these people are not Americans they shouldn't be here. If they don't like to be Americans they should go back to Africa'" (*Sentinel* "Board Recommends UC Regents Conduct Hearing on Black College," 9/ 10/68). The next month, Lans leveled allegations against Moore that he had threatened her life ("Two Claim Lives Threatened By Black Liberationists," 10/9/68).

Chancellor Dean E. McHenry refused to lend his support to the proposal, citing disagreement with Moore's belief that UCSC was Anglocentric. He claimed important steps were being taken to recruit "minorities" to the university and that many courses already were in existence that addressed the particular issues of people of color.

McHenry's refusal to represent the proposal to the UC

Regents (who decide the names of the various colleges) was based on a number of points. First, that the applicant pool of "qualified" minority professors was so small that such a program would be unsupportable. Second, that the hiring policies of such a college would be unconstitutional, in that it violated the 1964 Civil Rights Act. Third, that accepting a demand from the community would be an infringement of the academic autonomy and freedom of the university (*Sentinel,* "McHenry: Black College Not Practical," 9/15/68). The following day, McHenry gave a resolute "no" to the demands, stating among other things that the "'Black Experience· is too narrow a base for a possible theme of a college'" (*Sentinel,* "McHenry vetoes 'black' college," 9/16/68) and further that such a narrow scope would tend to "indoctrinate" students in a South African "Aparthied" like situation (*City on a Hill.* "College Seven," 11/15/68). A few months later, in similar statements, he responded to the demand for African architecture by stating that on his recent trip to Africa he observed no distinctive African style of architecture, the best buildings in Africa being American embassies; the result of American architects (*City on a Hill.* "Chancellor responds to CEP proposal." 1/31/69).

The BLM responded to this by refuting the idea that the college would be a black separatist institution. Rather, the BLM reasserted that the college would be open to students of all races, because The Black Experience, is a shared experience.

In an attempt to pacify the BLM, the general black community, faculty, and other students who had come out in support of the proposal, McHenry suggested alternatives to the proposed Malcolm X College, none of which met the demands articulated by the BLM. Responding to this, Moore stated, "The Black Community knows about compromise until what they are given has lost all meaning. One-twentieth of a university in the entire college system is enough of a compromise'" (*City on a Hill*, "College Seven proposals explained," 11/15/68). Interestingly, none of these alternatives carried the name of Malcolm X. To McHenry's suggestion that blacks be satisfied with a proposed Merrill curriculum that would stress ethnic studies, and a College 6 curriculum that would stress urban studies, Moore responded. '"We're being given tokenism... This shows signs of a racist mentality'" ("Chancellor responds to CEP proposal." 1/31/69).

That McHenry responded to the student demands was an indication that he felt pressure to maintain campus order, due to a Regent's meeting on the UCSC campus scheduled for 17th, and 18th of October. Two days prior to their arrival. William Moore was scheduled to speak at a meeting for the Student Mobilization Committee (SMC), but his speech was canceled by McHenry who feared his speech would excite the students on the eve of the Regents· arrival. Nonetheless, at the invitation of Ralph Abraham, a mathematics professor and campus radical, Moore spoke about the proposed goals of a Malcolm X College as a non-violent revolutionary step in education (*City on a Hill*, "Speaker defies Chancellor," 10/18/68).

McHenry reacted by banning the sponsoring group, the SMC, from campus activities, for violating school assembly regulations that non-student speakers must be approved by the chancellor's office, and that campus facilities cannot be used without official permission. The ban was lifted only after Ralph Abraham said that Moore had been his guest (*City on a Hill*. 11/8/1968).

The following day, Moore was barred from UCSC, by order of Dean McHenry, for the duration of the Regent's visit (10/17-18). The ban stemmed from Moore's disruption of a financial meeting conducted by the Regents, where the BLM representative voiced his support for the College of Malcolm X. To accomplish the removal. McHenry invoked the Mulford Act that allows campus officials to remove any non-student suspected of causing a disturbance (*Sentinel*. "UCSC Students To Support Malcolm X College plan", 10/29/68). Such was the political climate at the time, that infringements on the freedom of assembly and speech on college campuses were common occurrences.

Upon arrival, the Regents were met with widespread student dissatisfaction. Nearly one thousand students and twenty faculty, led by Paul Lee and Ralph Abraham, marched to the Crown courtyard to voice their dissatisfaction with university policies at a meeting of the Regents. Other faculty present were Smith, Jasper Rose and Noel King. Central to their demands were the reversal of impending and existing campus wide policies infringing on the political and academic freedom of students and faculty[6] (among these disallowing guest lecturers from appearing more than once a quarter-effectively destroying Eldridge Cleaver's inclusion in Stevenson courses 42 and 192), an official endorsement of the UFW grape boycott, and the acceptance of the proposal for Malcolm X College. In a partial victory, the Regents agreed to discuss the proposition for the college at their next meeting at UC San Diego. Of the Regents William Colentz was the most vociferous in his support of the student rally (*City on a Hill*." Regents to consider ... meeting," 10/18/68).

According to Lee, Moore made a trip to the university to speak with the Regents in spite of the ban, and was removed by campus police. Wally Goldfrank and Paul Lee retrieved Moore, who had been dropped off at the bottom of the campus by the police, bringing him back to the campus where they proceeded from the parking lot at Merrill to the demonstration at Crown. On their way, Rich Townsend, the leader of the Black Student Union, approached them and said that a few Regents were waiting for Moore at the Crown library to discuss the BLM's proposal for College Seven. Lee said: "Without breaking stride, Wally, William, Rich, and I, linked arms and marched into the library where three or four receptive Regents were waiting to talk to Bill."

Regents acting independently revealed to me that seemingly monolithic institutions contained competing strains, on one side the maintenance of the status quo, on the other the attempt to change the system from within. The more liberal Regents were willing to engage Moore in a dialogue about the possibility of a black studies college, thus showing good faith, albeit in a clandestine or private fashion. This division caused me to reconsider my previously held belief that large bureaucratic institutions are necessarily racist. It is not the institutions, but rather those that create and interpret policy that are racists. With this, the division between traditional liberals and conservatives, represented by McHenry, and radicals, represented by Abraham and Lee, was made clear. Moore enlisted the help of Lee and others as members of the academic institution who could work from the inside to change the system. McHenry, representing the bureaucracy, represented institutional resistance to change.

What is strange about McHenry's actions was that he considered the silencing of Moore as the key to maintaining order. For the chancellor, Moore was the symbol of unrest. Lee asks, "why scapegoat a black man for this role? Is it simply because he spoke the day before?" While both Lee and Abraham were singled out by McHenry for disciplinary action, they were not chosen as representatives of unrest. A black man was chosen for that role.

Paul Lee believed there was a two-fold anticipation

of Newton in Santa Cruz: Moore writing his History of Consciousness dissertation on Malcolm X, using Erik Erikson's unpublished work on a theory of the great man, that Erikson had given Lee at Harvard and, at the same time, Erikson's discussion of politics and psychology with Newton at Yale, a conversation which was published later — *In Search of Common Ground*. As Lee said, "And then comes Huey as if Bill and I had done our study program to prepare for his coming using Erikson as a key to Malcom X. It all seemed providentially arranged."

Chapter Two:
Newton's History at UC Santa Cruz

When Huey Newton applied to UCSC in late 1972, he had been planning a course of study with J. Herman Blake, the founding provost of Oakes College. Lee was able to become Newton's faculty advisor after Blake dropped out of the picture "... because of a conflict over royalties he thought Newton owed him as a result of his part in editing Newton's autobiography." Lee hesitated over the anticipated troubles Newton would encounter, but nevertheless agreed to take Newton through his BA program, "even if that meant hundreds if not thousands of steps to make it through the labyrinth of the obtuse bureaucrat. Especially in respect to someone like Huey."

Anticipating extreme reactions to his proposal to study at UCSC, Huey Newton's application included with it various reassuring letters of recommendation from distinguished individuals, including J. Herman Blake, UCSC professor Lewis Keizer, President of Merritt College Norvel Smith, Congressional Representative Ronald Dellums, and UC Berkeley professor Franz Schumann. (Appendix 3)

It was generally thought that because of Huey Newton's celebrity status, and the fact that he always traveled with a bodyguard and a secretary, his wife Gwynn, it would be easier to conduct the classes away from the campus. Lee went out of his way to accommodate Newton by organizing it so that Newton could take many of his courses (independent studies as well as individual and group seminars) in Lee's home at the base of campus. Among the professors to give Newton instruction at Lee's home were Noel King, Art Pearl, and Burney LeBoeuf, all of whom were very supportive of this individualistic program.

Huey Newton's undergraduate courses included diverse subjects, with Religious Studies, Biology, and courses on social movements and organization being the focus of his work. Paul Lee said that Newton enjoyed the program that took only one year, and that everything went very well, with Newton completing "extremely distinguished work," despite taking as many as five courses at a time (Appendix 4). In 1974 Newton received his BA in an independent major in Intercommunalism (education).

Newton immediately applied to the History of Consciousness Board for their Ph.D. program and was accepted on the basis of his academic achievements. Before he was able to enroll, he fled the country for fear of being incarcerated on charges of beating his tailor and killing a prostitute, incidents which allegedly occurred in Oakland. In November of 1974, Newton and Gwynn escaped to Cuba where they spent three years, with Newton working as a car mechanic (Johnny Chesko, taped interview).

Newton only came back to the United States after he was convinced that the political climate was such that his trial would be fair. Both charges were eventually dropped for lack of evidence.

Upon return, Newton re-enrolled in the doctoral program at UCSC and was welcomed back by many of his former professors as well as a few new ones, including Robert Trivers. Lee remained an advisor, although he had been removed from the university, having been denied tenure. Page Smith had resigned in protest, although he also continued to advise Newton as an emeritus professor.

Newton approached his individualistic interdisciplinary curriculum with zeal, enjoying high regard from professors in diverse fields such as Religion, Biology and the social sciences, who saw him approach his work with intensity, dedication and expertise.

Newton's doctoral dissertation, entitled *War Against the Panthers: A Study of Repression in America*, was an historical account of the FBI's counter-intelligence program (COINTELPRO) designed to cause the collapse of the Black Panther Party by illegal means. The most remarkable fact about the thesis was that most of the material documenting J. Edgar Hoover's attempt to destroy the BPP was derived from government sources. Newton had acquired the documentation through the Freedom of Information Act in the form of 8,000 250 page volumes (2,000,000 pages), 80% of which was aimed at the BPP (p.11). The dissertation was accepted and Newton graduated with a Ph.D. in 1980. The sheer volume of the documentation led Lee to label Newton as, "*the most hounded man in the history of mankind, as documented by the hounders*,"

Chapter Three:
Newton Meets the Faculty

While it is understandable that representatives of the white power structure would react negatively to the empowering nature of Newton's Marxist political line and militant self-defense approach, it is strange that he generated as much hateful energy from the white, "liberal" and academic communities of this country, the very segment of the population that is so quick to glorify the achievements of Dr. Martin Luther King Jr., another great human rights hero of the time.

As discussed in the Preface, my first encounter with a "revolutionary" academic at the University of California at Santa Cruz, Dr. Roberto Crespi, lead to his making negative assertions about Newton himself and the Party in general. I had enrolled in his course in "Revolutionary Literature" in the fall of my freshman year. I was informed by him that my intention to write a research paper on Newton and the BPP was not acceptable, because Newton was the person he least respected from the black liberation movement. Apparently Crespi didn't think Newton was worthy of my or his attention and stated matter-of-factly that he was a "rapist" and a "killer." In typical fashion, Crespi's comments blamed the victim of massive repression, Newton, for various alleged crimes.

The second time I heard about Newton in reference to his time at UCSC was after his death in August, 1989 in an article published in the *Santa Cruz Sentinel* newspaper. Dr. Gary Lease, a professor in the History of Consciousness program, made a comment with racist overtones when he referred to Newton as an "800 pound gorilla." Lease went further to describe Newton as a mediocre student, a non-intellectual and a misogynist, claiming that Newton treated his wife like a "bauble."[7] Lease went so far as to say that Newton did not deserve his Ph.D., because he had bullied his way through the program as well as the system and was not an intellect deserving of such a credential ("'The Man' at UCSC: passion and mediocrity," 8/23/89).[8]

When I first approached Dr. Hayden White, a professor
in the History of Consciousness, for an interview, similar
attitudes towards Newton were revealed. He had a very low
opinion of Newton in general, stating that, "Huey was already
down hill when he came here." White referred especially
to Newton's intimidatingly "violent nature" and alleged
criminal activities, speaking of both as if they were confirmed
fact. It was strange to hear White recall Newton's doctoral
dissertation, *War Against the Panthers: A Study of Repression
in America*, which was about the covert FBI manipulation of
events and their representation in the media, without any clue
to the irony of talking about the seemingly unquestionable
"criminal nature" of Newton.

When I started recording our conversation, he switched
gears and spoke of Newton in more general and moderate
terms. Turning from venom to honey, he prefaced the
interview by describing Newton and other black political
figures, most notably Angela Davis, as victims of institutional
prejudice and media harassment. "They are continually being
hassled ... people are making things doubly difficult for them
... so they become aggressive in return." He went on to say
that, "[Newton] wasn't overtly intimidating. He was always
polite and eager to demonstrate his interest in learning."

Later in the interview, White's facade eroded and the
negativity earlier expressed was revealed on tape. From
what I gathered, he had little knowledge of Newton or the
issues that surrounded his academic and/or political life and
apparently he had no desire to become aware of the issues,
which was revealed to me. He said, "I really don't know the
details [about Newton's legal turmoils] and frankly I don't
care." His lack of caring extended to general issues concerning
Newton in contemporary campus life; as an example he stated
that he had no knowledge of the annual Huey P. Newton

Memorial Lecture at Merrill College or the recent media backlash surrounding the event, led by the right wing student paper called the *Redwood Review*. In fact, White denied any knowledge of the existence of the *Redwood Review*!

While White taught only one course on either existentialism or the philosophy of history to Newton (he could not remember), he acted the expert and had these general things to say of Newton as a student,

> "Newton did satisfactory work. He really wasn't interested in learning. I think he thought he pretty much knew history from his own experience ... I have the idea that he wanted to show me that he was a very engaged student, but it was also evident that he was a guy who could figure out things very quickly. Oftentimes my feeling was that he did not work his way through the material. A lot of time was spent trying to bring him back ... [to the material]"

Members of the UCSC community who had more intimate contact with Newton saw him in a different light than Lease, White and Crespi. As described by Dr. Ralph Abraham, a professor of mathematics, Newton was, " ... a brilliant mind ... [and] a very misunderstood intellect" (interview, 1990). Dr. Page Smith, perhaps the nation's premier American historian and founding provost of Cowell College, described Newton as "... an eccentric genius" ('The Man' at UCSC 8/23/89). In an undergraduate evaluation, Dr. Burney LeBoeuf, the resident expert on the mating habits of elephant seals, declared, "Huey was undoubtedly one of the most stimulating students I have ever taught. I learned as much, if not more, from him as he learned from me" (Appendix 4). Reactions to his graduate work were even more flattering. Robert Trivers, a professor in sociobiology and later friend and colleague, described Newton as "... a genius ... a brilliant student-by far the brightest graduate student I've come across at this place." White expressed his resistance to working under the nonstandard conditions required for a student of Newton's stature. 'You don't want to try to deal with a student who has got an armed bodyguard sitting there, who has a reputation for violence ...there's a kind of symbolic intimidation going on there ...it was like having a movie star in your class ...That's not learning, that's not scholarship." White went on to joke about Newton's celebrity status, comparing Newton's disruptive presence to that of Jodie Foster at Yale, saying that, "... he was a media personality ... famous, glamorous with a Mercedes Benz and expensive suits."[9] White explained away his duplicity in Newton's icy welcome to UCSC, legitimizing his resistance to accommodate Newton by adopting the flock mentality that, "Many faculty felt that way."

Contrary to what Hayden White led me to believe, his contact with Newton was far from minimal. Paul Lee, one of Newton's faculty advisors, went so far as to say that White tried to thwart Newton's academic progress by repeatedly rejecting his paper on Existentialism. "There was a fear that White would flunk Huey and he would be ineligible as a Ph.D. candidate. This was the last class Huey had to pass." Lee went on to say, "I knew more about the subject than Hayden White, so I gave Huey a number of classes on the subject and introduced him to material White would not have known about," *e.g.*, the 75 pages of notes by Kierkegaard of Schelling's famous Berlin Lectures (1841-42), which Lee's teacher, Paul Tillich, called the "ur-text of Existentialism." Lee's philosophy teacher at St. Olaf, the renowned translator of Kierkegaard, Howard Hong, had sent Lee a copy of his translation of these notes. "A few more plums like that forced White to back off and pass Huey." Rather sadly, Lee went on to say that education is at a point where the writer must conform to the prejudices of the reader in order to succeed.

Commenting on the resistance that Newton faced, Dr. Robert Trivers, who worked extensively with Newton and taught him sociobiology, noted that Newton's fame caused people to view him differently and unfairly,

> " ... people had a hard time dealing with his fame and his reputed violent inclinations ... the whole association of Panthers with guns ...I remember him telling me, somewhat bitterly, about some professor here that told him in class not to bring guns on campus ... he found it highly offensive that this was said to him in class and furthermore, it was not true. There were never any guns on campus."

Many of the difficulties that professors had with Newton can be attributed to what Trivers describes as "... an ego problem that is rampant in academia." Trivers told me that upon meeting new professors, Newton would give them copies of his four books as a gift. Instead of accepting the gift graciously, many were intimidated and/or jealous of his success. They saw the gift as an arrogant gesture on Newton's part, as many of them had never published anything outside of scholarly journals.

Robert Trivers was made acutely aware of the negative relationship between Newton and the bureaucracy when Newton came to Trivers with the complaint that his academic folder was filled with inappropriate, non-academic materials, such as articles indicating his "criminality." While I did gain access to a copy of Newton's academic folder, I was not allowed to see the original so I have no way of verifying this claim.

Chapter Four:
Institutional Resistance to Newton

William Moore indicated that the established academics' reaction to Newton was due to the fact that he would not act the subservient and unchallenging student. Instead, with the help of a few receptive faculty members under the direction of Lee, Newton created his own program.

Where White saw a burden in Newton's demand for more attention, Moore saw an exciting challenge. Moore described his time with Newton as the most exciting in his life. He said, "Huey's academic experience was something that I found very [challenging]... one day you're having a shrimp salad or something ... and the next day you are in a courtroom and people are talking serious business ... and it went on like that for two or three years."

While Lee and many of his associates were excited by Newton's arrival, other teachers indicated their ambivalence towards Newton. This was especially so when he returned from Cuba. William Moore, who was at a meeting of the acceptance committee of the History of Consciousness, said many faculty attempted to bar his re-entry into the doctoral program. Among the reasons expressed by faculty was his reputed "violent" nature. Other faculty met his request for re-admision with the question, "What does he want here-to publish another book or something?" Moore said he was faced with similar 'bullshit" questions when he enrolled in the same program a few years earlier, indicating that such questions were typical of those posed to all African Americans.

Moore attributed the resistance to change to the

entrenchment of "... a bunch of pseudo intellectuals who sit in the classroom and play with education, correct papers, and walk through the trees and talk, talk, talk ..." He felt that many, but not all, college professors were not willing to put their "ass on the line," because they are in the pursuit of retirement, not truth, "...especially in terms of Third World people, poor people."

It was a classic case of a divided faculty, the bureaucracy (conservatives and traditional liberals) in power trying to do all they could to maintain the system as it was by denying Newton entry, and the radicals doing all they could to spice up their dying spirits by accepting Newton into their program and lives.

Lee explained why he and the other professors would go so far out of their way to accommodate Newton. "Huey presented himself in our context as a world leader with an intellectual ability that went with it and that's how we received him. He wasn't just a student, he was a major historical figure and he commanded immense interest and respect."

Page Smith explains his reasons for taking Newton on, in *Killing the Spirit*. In this book, Smith defines genuine teaching as the active pursuit of taking chances. Only when the teacher steps down from the dias and relates to the student on equal footing, so as to be vulnerable, can this be accomplished. Dialogue comes at the expense of social stature which is the recipe for real learning: "No professional vulnerability, no real teaching" (p.216). The old, in fact, can learn from the young.

Page Smith revealed to me what he believed to be the university's institutional resistance to anyone who was not willing to "get with the program" as defined by academia. Newton was an energetic student, oftentimes bringing his own lived experience into the classroom. This led to conflicts between Newton and his professors, who didn't think his personal history was, in Smith's words, "the right stuff academically speaking." Smith, however, believed that Newton's thesis, "an immediate social and political issue" which was the history of the repression of the BPP, was "a respectable and legitimate enterprise," or he says, "I wouldn't have done it" (i.e., served on Newton's thesis review committee). But he agreed that by History of Consciousness academic standards it may have been marginal going on to say that the non-academic aspect of Newton's work was one of the things that was most attractive about it. Smith confirmed Paul Lee's description of Newton as a world historical figure that commanded great respect, especially in radical circles and the black community.

Page Smith then told me why he took on such a potentially difficult student,

> In *Killing the Spirit*, I wrote that the academic world does not want passionate speech [the very essence of Newton's work] and is very suspicious and wary of any connection to real life. It's a strange and artificial world at the academy. They are very uneasy about anything that comes in and is ... disruptive and passionate and undisciplined. Newton was all of these things ... I suppose there was some sense of sticking it to the academy in my espousal or sponsoring of Huey's work. (My thinking was) You might not like this, but it's good for you. But it didn't make any difference. They just didn't like it!

Newton's presence required that traditional academics question the very foundation of teacher/student alienation, by insisting on a highly individualistic program. Newton essentially required that teachers pull away from their work and deal with him.

It should be reiterated that the individual attitudes of some professors towards Newton were not always a reflection of their ambivalence towards him, but rather a refusal to work outside the bureaucratic guidelines set forth by academia. The very structure of a bureaucracy works to dehumanize institutions, manifested by the alienation of students from teachers. However, I will say that certain faculty are guilty of adopting university policy as their own by reflecting resistance to special needs. As such, Newton's case points out something problematic about the modern bureaucratic university.

Chapter Five:
Newton vs. the Campus Marxists

Newton's arrival at UCSC gave many inactive Marxists a first hand look at a living revolutionary. One would think that Newton would have been warmly welcomed by the established Marxists on campus as a figure of historical significance to their causes. But this was not the case.

Paul Lee believed he was doing both Dr. Norman O. Brown and Huey Newton a favor when he arranged for the two to meet in his home. Lee described the meeting between an academic Marxist (Brown) and a political Marxist (Newton), who had an ability to discuss politics on an academic level, as a "flowering ... [which was one of] the greatest intellectual treats of my life." What Lee didn't notice at the time was that he was witnessing an encapsulation of the antagonisms that can occur when a representative of the school of thought and a representative of the school of action meet. Later, when asked to help sponsor Newton's graduate work in the History of Consciousness, Brown refused to work with Newton, claiming he was "far too dangerous. Count me out, count me out", he said. Since then, Lee has always referred to him as "Norman O. Brown nose."

The key to understanding this antagonism can be boiled down to two things, jealousy and fear. Newton was an easy target for Marxist academics because of the nature of his life's work: he put theory into practice. As a "dialectical materialist," he subjected their ideal to the test of reality and offended their "bookish" fundamentalism. For academic Marxists, who are forever entwined in the "correct" ideological preparation for action (to the point of social paralysis), Newton's activity represented a harsh reminder that they had "sold out." 'True prophets do not finish up between soft covers on expensive coffee-tables nor do they find themselves maintained in luxury by the great ones of the world; they tend to find themselves driven back into the desert, or dying on a gibbet, or severed from their heads which are borne upon silver platters to the paramours of the great" (Nicholl, "Restoration of Kinship," *Saturday Newspaper*). Newton represented something quite different — putting one's own life on the line and accepting one's own death as a prerequisite for revolutionary activity: "revolutionary suicide."

Most "historical Marxists" (as Newton called Marxist academics in his books) were especially displeased that the BPP sought to organize the "lumpen proletariat" (the underclass), because in so doing, the Marxist academic has no role in the revolution. Dialectical materialism left the BPP vulnerable to critiques by Marxist academic fundamentalists who could remain "true" to their vision of Marx only by virtue of the fact that their ideas never went further than the shelves of the library. Where Newton represented real life courage, Marxist academics represented intellectual hypocrisy. But Newton did not help smooth out the matter. Instead, he openly attacked them, not only by his presence, which was a constant reminder of their inadequacies, but also in his books. He clearly states in *To Die for the People*, that to not act on phenomena is to be an armchair philosopher (p.101). Tolstoi's words, it is easier "to write ten volumes of philosophy than to fulfill one of the precepts" concurs with this position (Nicholl).

The reaction of Marxist academics to Newton can be construed as professional jealousy aimed at an "active" revolutionary from the comfort of a faculty lounge in the Ivory Tower. The heads of state of China, North Korea and North Vietnam considered Newton the primary leader of black liberation and an important and essential part of Marxist world revolution. His brainchild, the BPP, was considered the vanguard party by radical feminist groups, gay liberation groups, Yippie groups, as well as established political entities like the Peace and Freedom Party and the Revolutionary Communist Party of America as well as a national threat by the federal government. Yet Marxist academics were barely considered by anybody. His academic career and later fall from grace was an opportunity for them to save a little face. Many used Newton's academic work to criticize the man. Others used the man to criticize the Party. Still others used the Party to criticize black people. All of this criticism resulted in material which resulted in more articles and a feeling of superiority for academic Marxists who were not required to act, but to think.

Newton's very presence was a constant reminder to academics that they had become part of the system. Newton frightened them, because, by making their precious ideas real, he was a threat to the position that they held in society. As university employees, academic Marxists have a vested interest in avoiding the revolution and maintaining the status quo. As members of an educational elite, they would necessarily be the victims of a revolution of the lumpen proletariat; thus Newton's activity becomes "dangerous." Marxist professors don't need the revolution because they are placed outside of conflict resolution and the hardships of life by virtue of the nature of their employment. They don't call for revolution now, but rather "... write obscure articles and books analyzing various aspects of capitalist culture with a view of some distant revolutionary event" (Smith, p.280). As such they accept no responsibility for the current state of affairs, because the revolution must first take place before they can change their immediate surroundings. So in the meantime they write bitter articles that focus on the "counter-revolutionary," "reformist" or "reactionary" actions of others who choose to act now; thus perpetuating their own jobs with the creation of endless documentation of the failures of others. And as we know, mere thoughts have no consequences. As Nicholl wrote, "... there is no connection between word and deed, between thought and action."

Erikson identifies the fundamental differences between men of thought and men of action when discussing and praising the differences between himself and the younger Newton,

> There are at least two kinds of experiences which separate men like him from men like me — the experience of violence in a largely hostile world and the experience of being totally captive, endless days and nights in solitary confinement. Huey has demonstrated a superhuman will under such conditions to keep the body vigorous, the mind alert and the soul open for new human experience (*In Search of Common Ground*, p.50).

Paul Lee said that, "Even if he was defamed here, he was an internationally renowned Marxist theoretician and dialectician ... He was up and above the professors at the Ph.D. level. He was involved in the 'real' world, a world-wide Marxist movement. He engaged in a dialogue inaccessible to them ... making real what professors were merely talking about and that threatened them" (interview, 1990). Dr. William Moore, another advisor to Newton, believed that few professors who encountered Huey could see too far beyond the 'book world," seconded this analysis.

The self-deception rampant in academia comes out of the separation of thought and deed: the illness of academia. The lack of a concrete application of ideas has led us to the edge of self-destruction. Newton reminded them of the evils of society and their unwillingness to dispose of them. "Newton put everything on the line," Moore said. "He not only jammed educational institutions, he jammed the system, so to speak, and that troubled people."

Chapter Six:
The Arrest — Newton's Character on Trial

Newton's reputation for violence was seemingly confirmed when Newton, William Moore, and Newton's bodyguard, Robert "Big Man" Heard were arrested in Aptos on May 10, 1978. Moore was released after posting bail of $25,000, but was never brought up on charges. Heard and Newton, on the other hand, were charged with assault with a deadly weapon, assault with an attempt to murder and being ex-felons[10] in possession of firearms. Heard's bail was set at $25,000 and Newton's at $60,000 (although bail of $200,000 was requested by the prosecution).

What is ironic about the events surrounding the incident at

the Mediterranean bar is the close connection that the events have to his dissertation, *War Against the Panthers A Study of Repression in America*. In aiding Newton with the project, Lee was amazed at the efforts expended by the federal government to destroy Newton and the BPP. Newton had secured more than 2,000,000 pages of FBI documentation via the Freedom of Information Act detailing the interdepartmental effort to discredit and otherwise destroy enemies of the federal government, most notably the BPP, especially through the misrepresentation of the BPP in the media (Newton, *War Against the Panthers*. p. 11).

Moore offered his interpretation of the events of that night to illuminate the actual chain of events of the evening, and in Moore's words, illustrate the "... magnitude of the system that [we] live under and the forces that can be brought against [us]" Moore saw the arrest as symptomatic of the forces that were brought against Newton, whose presence, either physical or intellectual, always seemed to elicit extreme reactions, both positive or negative.

On their way from Santa Cruz to Oakland, Moore, Newton, and Heard decided to stop for Mexican food at Manuel's Restaurant. The restaurant was closed, but they were given chips and dip and directed to the neighboring Mediterranean bar in hopes of getting some food.

Within a few minutes, Newton, Moore and Heard, were involved in a brawl sparked by the punch of a regular. At that point, a gun was fired two times, clearing the place, at which point Newton, Heard and Moore, left the scene. Once outside, they saw a police car, but the officer inside paid them no notice. They proceeded to get into Moore's car and depart the scene for fear of being attacked a second time. Soon after, Moore saw the red lights of the police cars and he ordered Newton and Heard out of the car, because, "... with Huey's

reputation and my reputation in Santa Cruz and of course
Bob, it was thought that this was the best move, because
if they catch us all in one car they're gonna blow us away."
Moore remained in the car and was approached by a police
officer who pointed a 357 magnum revolver (not general
issue) at his head and yelled, "If you fuckin move I'm gonna
blow your head off." Moore was then arrested, as was Heard,
who was hiding his 300+ pound frame behind a "two foot
branch," and finally Newton, who was found in an open field
not far from the car. The three men were then taken to the
police station and jailed, after which Moore was checked for
alcohol or drug usage. He tested negative. The police had
wanted blood and urine samples from all three men, but
Moore insisted that only he be checked due to the fact that
only he was operating the vehicle at the time of arrest. Once
in jail the guards attempted to give the Newton group special
privileges, which they interpreted as an attempt to pit them
against the other inmates. They refused to take the special
treatment.

The attitudes expressed by the *Sentinel* undermined
journalistic objectivity in every article about the arrest. Each
story carried with it an indictment of Newton, in the form
of his rap sheet of alleged criminal activities, among them
the shooting death of a prostitute (at the time he was free on
$80,000 bail) and the beating of his tailor, both in Oakland in
the early '70's. Newton was never convicted of either crime. By
casting Newton as having a history of lawlessness, his role as
instigator in the fight was assumed.

When the case came to court, the attitudes of the
prosecution were revealed. Assistant District Attorney Ralph
Boroff, over the objections of Newton's attorneys, questioned
Newton's character. He said that "'Mr. Newton undoubtedly
has the reputation in any community in America, to be

known as a violent person" (*Santa Cruz Sentinel*, "Judge Rules in Newton Case," 6/8/78), which set the tone of the case. This statement could only worsen public attitudes towards Newton as well as perpetuate community misconceptions of Newton and the BPP as being aggressively violent. Newton's guilt was assumed which the prosecution used to their advantage, sidestepping the basic legal process of innocence until proven guilty.

The press saw an opportunity to use Heard's physical characteristics to cast the defense as the aggressor. His physical characteristics were mentioned in twelve of fifteen articles mentioning his name, ranging anywhere from 6'8"-300 lbs. (10/30/79, 6/13/80) to 6'8"-350 lbs. (11/1/79) to 7'-300 lbs. (3/9/78) to 7'-350 lbs. (8/22/78). At the same time the weights of Newton, Moore, Hall or the police were not mentioned. Stressing the incredible physical characteristics of Heard served to insinuate aggressiveness and convince the reader of his super-humanness, in effect, de-humanizing him.

The unfair treatment of Heard included printing simple untruths that worked to convince the reader of his criminality, even after the trial had blown over. Faced with jail time stemming from the Santa Cruz weapons possession charge, Heard fled across country only to be caught a year later. When Heard was extradited to California, it was reported in the Sentinel that he was captured in Georgia after robbing a liquor store of $2,300 (12/18/79). In fact, no robbery had occurred and he was picked up in Florida (probably for the "crime" of being a large black man) in connection with the charges in Santa Cruz. Blaming the Associated Press for the "misinformation" the *Sentinel* offered no apology.

Surprisingly, even Boroff freely admitted that a fair trial for Newton was going to be difficult to achieve in Santa Cruz due to the extreme amount and nature of the press coverage

("Newton And Bodyguard Each Face Three Charges,"
5/11/78). But the events leading to his arrest didn't seem to
surprise Newton, who said, "When I go into court I always
expect the ridiculous" ("Newton Pleads Innocent," 5/26/78).

In another article, "Seacliff Bar Brawl: Newton arrested
in Shooting" (5/11/78), the *Sentinel* described a "minor
argument" that developed into a "melee" in which a Santa
Cruz man was shot. The testimonies of many eye-witnesses
were conflicting, placing the gun in the hand of either Heard
or Newton at the time that one of the men had fired a pistol at
Kenny Hall.[11]

The judge consistently sidestepped Newton's attorney's
objections that two key witnesses for the prosecution were,
"... people of disreputable character with a racial bias'"
(*Santa Cruz Sentinel*, "Newton Hearing Delayed," 6/5/78).
Documentation as to the prevalence of racist attitudes at
the bar was provided by the police report that quoted an
eyewitness to the scuffle as saying, "there's a couple of niggers
tearing up the place" ("No Guns, Newton Urged at Bar
Melee," 6/10/78). Furthermore, anti-Newton and anti-black
graffiti reading "'Hang Niggers'" and "'Kill Huey'" was found
in the bathroom of the bar, dated earlier than the incident,
indicating a history of tolerated race hatred at the location
("Newton Hearing Continued," 6/30/78).

The case began to smell of a conspiracy when the Sheriff's
Department failed to serve seven of twenty witnesses with
subpoenas, causing Newton's lawyer to believe that there had
been a violation of "due process" and that Newton was being
railroaded into jail ("Newton hearing Continued," 6/30/78).
The addresses of all but two witnesses were withheld from the
defense. Needless to say, the inability to contact 35% of the
witnesses severely limited the defense's ability to prepare for
trial. The information was withheld because an undisclosed

number of witnesses were supposedly contacted and threatened with violence by Newton if they chose to testify.

Speculation as to the genuineness of the calls, and the fact that the charges were not immediately dismissed could lead one to believe that the threats were the result of an FBI engineered, COINTELPRO-type maneuver. But the threats were attributed to Newton or his associates in a headline which read, "Newton posts Bail; Witnesses Threatened" (5/12/78) which further vilified Newton in the eyes of the general public. According to *Agents of Repression* attempts to vilify black leaders by means of the legal system was a common tactic. Hoover believed that projecting an image of "'Panther violence'" through the media would lend credence to the federal government's desire to see the Panthers cast as provocateurs, thus justifying their repression of the group. "While the FBI considered Federal prosecution a 'logical' result, it should be noted that key activists were chosen not because they were suspected of having committed or planning (sic) to commit any specific Federal crime'" (Churchill, Vander Wall, p.94). Knowing this, it is not surprising that Newton's attorney Floyd Silliman asked Kenny Hall, the supposed victim of the shooting, if he was or had ever been "... employed by the CIA or the FBI" when he took the stand ("Witness Testifies He Started A Fight With Newton," 7/7/78).

When the case came to court, interesting if not embarrassing truths, were revealed. First and foremost, Newton and his associates had not been the aggressors they were assumed to be. In fact, they had been jumped almost immediately after entering the bar. Second, there were two off-duty policemen who worked at the bar and one or both of them may have been there at the time. The embarrassment comes with the third point in connection with the second: that the bar was a notorious prostitute hangout. Fourth and finally, many of the patrons of the bar who provided testimonies had been at the bar for more than two hours and had been drinking to the point of intoxication. Newton and his associates had not had time to order drinks and were thus presumed to be sober. Interestingly, none of these facts were mentioned in the *Sentinel*.

On July 7, 1978, Hall came out and admitted having instigated the fight with Newton ("Witness testifies He Started A Fight With Newton"). Both bullets were found in the rafters of the bar, indicating that the weapon had been discharged pointed at the ceiling. Hall's injuries were determined to have occurred when Hall pushed Newton through a plate glass window. Even after this testimony, Newton and Heard faced weapons charges, although the charges against Newton were later dropped.[12] Heard ended up serving six months on a nine month sentence (Moore, interview).

So it was Newton, Moore and Heard who had been the victims of the attack, but because of their reputation for violence and the fact that they were black, it was assumed that they were the aggressors. It was a classic example of the victimization of people of color in a legal system that casts them as guilty until proven innocent.

It seems rather clear that the entire incident was a political trial. Rather defensively, in an article entitled, "Ex-Newton Bodyguard Sentenced" (12/18/79), Boroff insisted that Heard's affiliation with the BPP had no bearing or influence on the conviction. Moore sees things differently though, believing that Newton's and the BPP's reputation had a lot to do with the proceedings of the court and the media portrayal of events. According to Lee, before the facts were disclosed by the court proceedings, it was generally thought among people that Newton, Heard and Moore were guilty, that they had entered the bar "looking for trouble." In fact, the prosecution relied on that fact.

From the very beginning of the trial many involved in the court proceedings knew the charges were trumped up. Municipal Judge William Kelsey, who ordered the charges to be dropped "for lack of evidence," revealed that the only thing he was convinced of was "... that shots were fired in the Mediterranean that night." Newton's attorney, Silliman, explained, "it seems to me ... [their] case just fell apart" ("Newton's Lawyer Asks For Dismissal," 7/11/78).

But as in many of his previous encounters with the power structure, Newton suffered. Newton expressed his belief that even if he had been cleared of all charges, justice had not been served. "By charging me unfairly they have cost me bail premiums, attorney's fees and time out of school ... I'm out $30,000. If you call that justice, we have a different standard" ("Newton Cleared in Case," 7/14/78).

The condemnation of Newton and Heard in the *Sentinel* did not end with the charges being dropped. More than a year later, in "Huey Newton's Bodyguard Captured" (10/30/79), a staff writer took as truth the testimony of Kenny Hall that he had been shot by Newton in the bar with a gun handed to him by Heard. Likewise, the article fails to mention that Hall had admitted to starting the fight in which he pushed Newton through a plate glass window and cut his head. Most significantly, the article did not mention that both bullets were found in the rafters of the bar, indicating that the shots were fired at the ceiling and not at Hall ("Newton hearing Will Resume Monday," 7/9/78). In short, the article relied on the short-term memory of the reader and perpetuated Newton's negative characterization.

Moore speculated about the incident in relation to Newton's previous "problems" with the Law, "I know there were other incidents that Huey was involved with ... those I wasn't there for. This one I was there. I saw how people reacted — I watched it in the newspaper ... I found that if the rest of these stories that are in a negative light are as bullshit as this one then I got real serious doubts about the other [charges]."

Conclusion:
Why come to UCSC? — Newton's work as helping us understand Newton.

In Huey Newton's letter of intent to UCSC, he described his own educational experience as being typical of African Americans in the schooling process. A functional illiterate after graduating high school, Newton was told by a career counselor that he was not college material. Rising to the challenge, Newton, in prison, taught himself to read by reading again and again Plato's *Republic* (Gilbert Moore, *A Special Rage*, p. 40). With an uncanny intuition he picked the one tell in the history of western thought that historicizes the transition from the oral culture of Homer to the literate and rational self-conscious culture of Socrates. The letter continues by outlining the broad academic interests that he tackled at Merritt College where he received an A.A. degree, while at the same time continuing his "street" education; both of which figured in his founding of the Black Panther Party.

"[C]onstantly amazed by [people of the street's] abilities, their brilliance, and their unfulfilled potentials," Newton wanted to reach those who had traditionally been ignored by America's racist schooling system. Upon release from prison in '71 (on charges stemming from the alleged killing of John Frey), Newton saw his role as "Minister of Information" of the BPP, as the role of a teacher. He saw his own higher education as a step towards improving his own ability to think critically, which he hoped to pass on to others in the black community

(Appendix 1).

Newton stressed the importance that revolutionaries obtain bourgeois skills (such as a university education) to operate in a highly advanced, technological, bureaucratic society (*To Die For The People*, p.68.). Newton occupied the middle ground between those strict Marxists who called for revolutionaries to drop out of society, and those Marxists who had become part of the system through employment in capitalist institutions. In a speech by Bobby Seale, given at the Second Annual Huey P. Newton Memorial, he stressed that the BPP was not a reformist organization. The Party did not support those who had become part of a system that oppresses distinct socio-economic groups, but at the same time stressed that, 'You can't drop out of the system ... even if you go to the moon, Uncle Sam is going to drag you back because he's already been there" (2/26/91).

When I asked Page Smith about Huey Newton, he seemed puzzled by the question as to why a man of such obvious stature and renown would want to attend the University of California at Santa Cruz. He couldn't see what interest a man of Newton's accomplishments could gain from a university education. In general, Smith has a very bad impression of Ph.D.'s, calling doctoral programs "a cult of dullness" (Smith, p.110). Smith offers us Ionesco's *The Lesson* as a metaphor for higher education. A female student enters the classroom as the teacher lectures on the etymology of Spanish verbs. Suffering from a toothache, she attempts to interrupt the teacher. When she gets so loud as to disturb the lesson he kills her, at which point, another student enters (p. 218). The main point of the play is captured in Smith's offering of a Eugen Rosenstock-Huessy quote that, "Present day teaching is a series of farewell parties to life" (p.123).

Speaking about the student activism in the university

during the '60's and '70's he writes that "... they were scolded for breaking the rules of civilized academic discourse and then, figuratively speaking, they were killed" (p.173). What annoyed some of Newton's professors more than anything else was that no matter how hard they tried to bend him to their system, he would not. He had built around him a constituency strong enough to shield himself from their attacks. When they moved to force Newton into the intellectual suicide of required courses and bureaucratic turmoils, they found themselves way too slow for the resourceful Newton who found great allies in Lee, Moore, Pearl and others.

But Smith couldn't understand why Newton would want to risk a dual suicide; first "revolutionary suicide" when one gives up the body to the cause, and second an intellectual suicide, a "reactionary suicide," when one gives up the mind for credentials.

William Moore attributed Smith's inability to understand Newton to a common perception of Newton as not having developed over time.

> "People used to see Huey with the gun as they did in the 60's, and where he was in the 70's and especially in the 80's wasn't a whole different person, but he had moved beyond that point [as is seen in his review of *Sweet Sweet Back* reconsideration of Black Capitalism in *To Die For the People*]. He still had no problems with ... defending the people ... but as an intellectual he had moved beyond that point and people just wanted to keep pulling him back ... like Godfather III ...They look at Huey and they still see the guy with the black jacket, the beret and the shotgun, and this guy's way down the line from there. He still has that experience ... under-

stands that ... knows about the jail, the system ... But
he was beyond that. And you gotta communicate
to him on that level. You can't typecast him and he's
supposed to play this role for you ... He wouldn't
give a shit who you are or who you think you are ...

A review of Huey Newton's course work at UCSC is
important in that it illuminates basic themes in the life of
Newton, while at the same time helping us understand the
man himself.

Biology: Deceit and Self-Deception

Newton took two courses from Robert Trivers, one on
"deceit and self-deception" and the other on "sociobiology."
Newton mastered both, especially the former. Trivers said
Newton was, "a master at spotting deception, propagating
deception and analyzing deception."

Trivers was especially impressed with Newton's ability to
digest and think through materials in fields he had little or
no experience with. Newton read everything Trivers gave
him, oftentimes making very "trenchant comments," spotting
things and interpreting things in a very different way than
Trivers. Trivers said Newton went "... beyond the usual level
that graduate students do ... discussing the latest theoretical
and empirical issues in my field almost as equals." Trivers was
so taken by Newton's work in the field that he invited Newton
to publish a book with him on the subject, with the material
generated from their seminar together. Although they
obtained a contract for the book and completed a first draft of
the manuscript, the book was never published.

It was a study of both animals and humans, with Trivers
taking frogs and Newton humans. The basic premise of the

book was that those who exercise power over others tend to be involved in a certain amount of self-deception, while others use deceit in order to survive, suggesting a tragic collusion between the two, under the theme of mimicry. In a *Santa Cruz Sentinel* article, Newton is quoted as saying, "I've suffered a lot of persecution and prosecution from the state, and to survive I've had to understand deception" ("Huey Newton, Prof Collaborate On Book About Deceit," 2/14/82).

Trivers explained that where deceit may help one's survival, self-deception is inherently harmful. "You're denying reality to yourself and you're crippling yourself." The self-deceiver denies him/herself reality thus denying access to information. Therefore, those involved in self-deceit are more likely to be deceived by others who recognize self-deception.

> People occupying society's upper echelons are in powerful positions and benefit from accurate information ...Those occupying lower echelons are disadvantaged and frequently gain from withholding information from their superiors and fabricating stories. (*Sentinel*. 2/ 14/82).

That Trivers wanted to pursue a co-authorship with Newton, coupled with the fact that Newton had done distinguished work with Erikson in one of his four books, should lay to rest the idea that Newton was intellectually mediocre.

Social Science: Repression

As has been explained, Newton's dissertation, *War Against the Panthers*, is essentially autobiography as history. It chronicles the rise of the Black Panther Party and the federal government attempts to destroy it as a viable political and social organization.

The FBI, as "agents of repression," served to protect the "natural order" that had been threatened by the promise of the BPP, which was the radical restructuring of American society to be true to the equality "guaranteed" by the U.S. Constitution. The agents who carry out this repression, seemingly in the name of law and order, are merely doing the dirty work of those who have a vested interest in the maintenance of the disparaging distribution of wealth and power in the world (p. 5).

Newton explains that the present balance of power in society is maintained through violence. By untruthfully portraying the BPP, through the media, as aggressively violent, the FBI effectively justified their illegal repression. The repression took the form of various control tactics, among them simple misrepresentation of the Party to the public, harassing legal battles, and outright assassination of Party members (pp. 6-7). Newton considered the ferocity of such repression was an indication of how dangerous the federal government saw the BPP to the present order (p. 126).

Newton points out in the dissertation that while the federal government maintains that the "violence" of the BPP was what incurred their wrath, the truth of the matter is that what most threatened Hoover was the "free breakfast" programs offered by the Party. The "free breakfast" represented to the federal government the biggest threat to society, because it was a threat to the very nature of bourgeois capitalism and "laissez fair" politics. The program encapsulated the most disturbing things about the Party; a "revolutionary ideology, community service, and a willingness to engage in legal struggle to achieve ... goals" (p. 126).

A Senate Select Committee (aka the Church Committee

after Idaho Senator Frank Church) compiled its *Final Report* in April 1976, describing the FBI's COINTELPRO tactics as "unworthy of a democracy and occasionally reminiscent of the tactics of totalitarian regimes" (p. 132). While the dissertation was a personal account, the materials used were derived from the *Final Report*, various scholarly studies, litigation between the BPP and the federal government, as well as media reports.

The irony of his work at UCSC was not lost on Paul Lee, Page Smith, William Moore and Newton himself. The hounded writes a thesis based on information provided by the hounders and is arrested by local police authorities in the process. His arrest in Santa Cruz showed the extent to which law enforcement agencies will go in order to remove threatening figures from society. Likewise, it provides a metaphor for Newton's time at UCSC where he confronted the bureaucracy. What resulted was a classical instance of an historical outsider becoming involved in an antagonistic contradiction with the established order at one of its smaller, but just as impenetrable, levels. He represented the marginal individual at odds with society, trying to get his due, and being subsequently run through the system. Newton's completion of his degree is a testimony to his perseverance and the loyalty of friends and colleagues; all in spite of the bureaucracy.

Religious Studies: Son of Man Theme

Newton took various classes in the Religious Studies department (then chaired by Gary Lease), most of which were independent seminars with Paul Lee and Noel King. Lee and King believed that Newton continued his career in higher education as it afforded him an opportunity to pursue his religious interests, which both believed were tied to his political ideology.

As the primary theoretician and dialectician of the Black Panther Party, Newton developed a Marxist-inspired theoretical framework for understanding socio-political phenomena. To describe this new theory he coined the term "revolutionary intercommunalism." The ideology of the Black Panther Party took an holistic approach to analysis in their connection to the struggles of all colonized people, especially black colonized people.

Newton recognized the U.S. as an empire with technological capabilities that made the entire world a community and subjected that world to what he identified as "reactionary intercommunalism" (the siphoning off of international resources for domestic prosperity). Newton steadfastly argued that this technology of destruction could be used to better the conditions of all oppressed peoples in communities throughout the world: thus revolutionary intercommunalism (*In Search of Common Ground*. p. 31).

A dialectical materialist. Newton believed in the organic nature of political ideologies; the natural progression from capitalism (nationalism) to socialism (internationalism) to intercommunalism (rise of the community in the place of the nation) to communism (no nation) and beyond. The final state of political awareness would then transcend the material world and people would move into a godly state, if not become god altogether. Newton phrases this succinctly in *In Search of Common Ground.*

> " ... imperialism negates itself after laying the foundation for communism, and communism will eventually negate itself because of its internal contradiction, and then we'll move on to an even higher state. I like to think that we will finally move

to a state called "'godliness," where man will know
the secrets of the universe-and when I say universe,
I mean all motion and matter" (p.33).

Newton explains this further on page 109, when he writes,

" ... after the dialectical process has run its
course, man will reach a state of godliness-and
that's because I think God is mostly what man has
said, 'I am not.'"

His vision was not limited to the future of celestial unity.
He explains on the same page his hopes for the future for all
mankind,

" ... dialectics would make it necessary to have
a universal identity. If we do not have a universal
identity, then we have cultural, racial, and religious
chauvinism, the kind of ethnocentrism we have
now ... we struggle for a future in which we will
realize that we are all Homo Sapiens and have more
in common than not."

Newton believed that "Unless we cultivate an identity with
everyone, we will not have peace in the world" (p. 67). It was
the purpose of the BPP schools to cultivate that universal
identity.

Noel King conducted an independent study for Newton
on the Jewish idea of the Son of Man. King explained that in
the Hebrew tradition, the Son of Man is a corporate identity
of man and woman, regardless of race; a universal expression
of human kind that is made manifest in the individual.
King said that Newton expressed these ideas in a twenty-

page paper that he pressed Newton to publish. In the paper,
Newton discussed various messianic themes of Christianity
as the fulfillment of the Son of Man tradition. It tied closely
to his idea of revolutionary intercommunalism in that it dealt
with the universality of humanity. In the Bible, this universal
expression of mankind is personified in Jesus the Christ, the
Messiah. The paper discussed Jesus's death as the realization
of a universal identity through reconciliation. His death ended
the estrangement between Jesus and God in that it cultivated a
feeling of atonement; oneness.

Huey Newton named the BPP survival schools, "The Son of
Man School." Knowing the theological aspect to his politics of
contradiction (dialectical materialism-intercommunalism)
this was not surprising at all. In fact, the theological bent
of Newton's work is what attracted many people to him,
including Smith, Lee, and King.

What is most interesting about Newton's "political
theology" is its autobiographical aspect. I must thank Paul
Lee for outlining the biblical material and illuminating the
metaphorical aspect of Newton's relationship to the Son of
Man theme — something which helps us understand Newton
and his vision of himself as a reconciler, and a leader.

Lee outlined the messianic expectations in terms of the title
"Son of Man" in the biblical times of Jesus:

> Of the messianic titles, Jesus referred to the Son
> of Man most often leading one to believe that it is a
> critical theme of the Messianic expectations. In the
> Gospel of Mark, Jesus does not refer to himself as
> the Son of Man, so the question arises as to whether
> or not Jesus thought of himself as the Son of Man.
> One gets the sense that Jesus believed there was an-
> other to come, so the Son of Man, the heavenly man

would someday come and deliver the Isrealites from the hands of the Romans and Jesus is the one who prepares the way just like John the Baptist prepared the way for him.

Having studied messianic themes extensively, Newton knew that,

The Son of Man is the First Adam, the Adam of Creation, not the Second Adam, the Adam of the Fall. This can easily be misunderstood, as the Apostle Paul refers to Jesus as the "second Adam," but he means *the second coming of the First Adam*, So the second coming of the first Adam (who is created in the image of God) is what Jesus refers to as the Son of Man; man with a capital "M" (a universal identity). The Son of Man is then the creature of unambiguous goodness who will come on the clouds as the Man from Above and deliver the faithful from their enemies (the Romans). Finding its roots in the Persian symbol of the "Original Man," the Son of Man is like Zarathustra, an apocalyptic figure who in the last eon will usher his people out of their worst bondage in to salvation, understood as an act of cosmic healing.

As developed in Paul Tillich's *Systematic Theology*, "The symbol 'Son of Man' ... designates an original unity between God and Man" (p. 109). Lee explained that,

In Mark, Jesus refers to someone who is to come after him, thus what John the Baptist is to Jesus, Jesus is to the Son of Man; which is to say that Jesus is preparing the way for the Son of Man. This original unity is expressed in the Creation account in Genesis 1-2:4 where man is created in the image of God.

Lee outlined Tillich's four fundamental steps in understanding christological symbols. The first,

> "... points to the historical/transhistorical figure through whom God will establish a kingdom in Israel and through Israel the whole world. The prophetic period is to the historical development as the transhistorical is to the apocalyptic. So at the time that the Romans have conquered them [the Israelites] time has come to an end. Everything is so bad that something is going to have to come and deliver them; hence, the mood of transhistorical apocalypticism.
>
> [The second is] the experience of Man's predicament ... [the realization that the] kingdoms are full of injustice and misery. The present society is in a state of decay and disease. Salvation is longer for because it brings in new vitality ... divine power. The roots of these motifs are in Persia and the Ancient World.
>
> [The third is] the reception and transformation of a set of symbols by Christianity. The Messiah who is supposed to usher in the new age is defeated by the powers of the old age as the Suffering Servant. The defeat of the Messiah on the cross is the most radical transformation of the symbol of the Messiah, so radical that Judaism denies the messianic character of Jesus; *a defeated Messiah is not a messiah at all.* Christianity acknowledges the para-

dox and accepts it.

[Fourth is the] literalistic distortion of the messianic paradox. The title of the Christ becomes a proper name and ceases to be the symbolic designation of a function. Christ became an individual with supernatural powers who through a voluntary sacrifice, and not all that voluntary made it possible for God to save those who believed in Him. The paradox disappeared" (Tillich, pp. 109-110).

Paul Lee explained what he thought to be the most important thing about Christianity as expressed in the New Testament,

Jesus *identifies* the Son of Man theme with the Suffering Servant of Isaiah (cf the so-called Servant Songs of Second Isaiah). So instead of being the Man from Above who overthrows the Romans, the symbol of the Son of Man is given a transvalued image as the Suffering Servant and the Messiah is *handed over to the enemy to be put to death by them.* This is the paradox, or, the contradiction against all expectations. The most animated argument between Jesus and the disciples is that Jesus accepts the paradox that the Son of Man is to undergo the fate of the Suffering Servant and suffer death upon the Cross. The Disciples reject this idea so harshly that they don't even want to talk to him anymore. In Mark, it is clear that Jesus is referring to somebody else, but slowly he realizes that the one he refers to is himself — he is destined to be the Son of Man/Suffering Servant: the Agony in the Garden of Gethsemane is Jesus' tearful effort to remove from himself this cup of suffering from which he does not want to drink his own blood.

Lee explained that this Christological theme for Newton becomes quite clear in that,

> Isaiah's vision of the Suffering Servant is that he will be the "ugliest of them all", in fact, a leper. The Suffering Servant then represents the most despised, the most rejected, the ugliest will be the Messiah. Therefore, Jesus knows that to be the Messiah is to be the defeated Messiah. The Messiah looks nothing like the Messiah, especially staked to a cross. The last will be the first and the first will be the last.

Lee, who taught under Tillich at Harvard divinity school, believed Newton had an uncanny intuition that the heart of the Son of Man theme was the paradox of his fate as the Suffering Servant. Newton understood that the Son of Man was the major christological symbol and he identified with that because of his understanding of his own life as already being over as a "revolutionary suicide."

Noel King believed that Newton saw the concept of the Son of Man in all of us and that only if we accept this role can we embark on the path to reconciliation. King believed that Newton saw himself as a reconciler attempting to bring back the concept of a universal identity.

While some would point to Newton's identification with the Son of Man as delusion, I would chalk it up to an inability to really understand Newton and what he meant to others as the "... administrative leader and chief ideologue of a movement, an important symbol to those who follow him and those who fear him, a man very much caught up in the historical currents he has helped set into motion" (*In Search of Common Ground*, p. 10).

In 1971, Lee first met Newton with Richard Baker, the former Abbott of the Zen Center in San Francisco and Gerd Stern who had come to know Newton through Bert Schneider, one of the principle financial contributors to the BPP. The theological aspect of their discussion was made dramatic by the fact that a Zen Buddhist Priest, a Hassidic Jew (Stern), a Protestant theologian (Lee) and a black revolutionary were the participants. Lee recalled his conversation with Huey Newton in our interview. What he remembers in particular is Newton's description of intercommunalism and how he was struck by the influence or at least the similarities to the Apostle Paul. Lee believed that the concepts, consciously or not, were straight out of the Bible. Lee described intercommunalism as an espousal of a biblical vision that amounted to a political theology. The Apostle Paul, in his highest vision of the Christian mysteries, says that "God will be all in all". This, for Lee, was implicit in Newton's vision of intercommunalism. Newton had a sense that intercommunalism is spiritual politics that can transcend national problems.

Outside of the fact that Newton referred to his school as the "Son of Man School," Newton's identification with the messiah, at least symbolically, was not generally known. Newton knew that a political theology would carry extreme weight in the black community, but he may have been unprepared to assume the role of a religious leader, although there was some suggestion that after his graduate work, he would study for the ministry. He would refer to the position of his being the 7th son as a sign of his calling.

While Page Smith was surprised that Newton came back to school, Paul Lee was surprised that Newton didn't go on to a theological seminary![13]

Moore said Newton's religious thoughts did not end in college. Moore spoke with Newton just before his death. He understood that Newton was going to become involved in religion by starting a church and becoming a minister which Moore felt made him "dangerous to people."[14] Moore speculated that this was perhaps a reason for his death.

Appendix 1
Huey Percy Newton

One of the most important aspects of my life has been education. Although I was born in Louisiana my family moved to Oakland while I was an infant and I have lived here all of my life. All of my learning, which has taken place in Oakland, has been a dual education.

My years in the public schools were very tumultuous. From elementary through high school I found myself continually in rebellion against the teachers and schools which I found to be very oppressive for Black youth. Without realizing it, I was trying to maintain my dignity and pride in this situation. As a result of this pattern of oppression and resistance I graduated from high school a functional illiterate.

Because of my rebelliousness when a high school counselor told me I was not college material I determined to enter college and do well just to prove to myself how wrong he was. To do this I spent a long painful summer teaching myself to read. Then I entered Merritt College in Oakland and eventually graduated with an A.A.

During my junior college experience I was also getting another education on the streets of Oakland. I spent many hours in the bars, pool rooms and street corners with many of my friends from high school who had moved into pimping, prostitution, narcotics and the other devastating forms of survival so many poor Blacks were forced to adopt. I was constantly amazed by their abilities, their brilliance, and their unfulfilled potentials.

In Merritt College I was studying philosophy, sociology, psychology and other subjects, but on the streets I was studying people. Eventually I merged these two interests and organized the Black Panther Party to provide the Black community with a' new method for resolving the problems we faced on the streets of Oakland. I wanted to teach the people who had never been reached by the educational system, not only by ideas but by examples. As a result of our work many of us have died and many of us have spent long years in prison. Bobby Seale, co-founder of the Black Panther Party, and I have both spent years in prison without conviction on a single charge. Yet we have braved this storm of opposition and now the Black Panther Party is stronger than ever, so I am now able to pursue my educational interests in another way.

When I was released from prison in August, 1970, I recognized that a crucial need among my comrades was the ability to think critically and creatively. I am called the chief theoretician of the Black Panther Party and I do develop many ideas for its Central Committee.· But I have begun to teach others how to do their own critical and creative thinking. This teaching has become a very important part of my life and I want to extend the emphasis on critical thought into the Black community far beyond the confines of the Black Panther Party.

Therefore I have returned to college to complete my education and move into graduate study. I am now attending Merritt College to make up deficiencies and I plan to enter UCSC to continue my studies with special emphasis on philosophy and also the social sciences. These areas of study are closest to my personal interests and goals.

I expect that in a few years the Black Panther Party will be riding the crest of the organizational movement now taking place in Black communities. I am preparing myself for the new developments which must come by completing my education. In the future I would like to teach in a junior college in the Oakland-San Francisco area.

Appendix 2

The Black Liberation Movement
P.O. Box 1502
Santa Cruz, California

August 18, 1968

Brothers & Sisters:

The University of Californian is in the process of electing some twenty (20) colleges on their campus at Santa Cruz, Calif. To date four (4) are complete.

On the night of August 7th, 1968. The Black Liberation Movement of Santa Cruz answered the question white America has posed to Black People for long time with a new reply — a revolutionary proposal which can be implemented now. That is:

1. The (seventh) 7th college built at UCSC — be Afro American — instructing in the "Black Experience".
2. This college be architecturally designed by an Afro American reflecting their heritage.
3. This college must be named Malcom X.

4. A forum room seating up to 250 people be open to the people, where the "Black Experience" will be expressed from 8 a.m. to 10 p.m. covering the whole spectrum of the people of color: African. Here the finest minds and talents of the People of Color will be expressed.

5. The degrees awarded will be:

    1. Bachelor of Afro-American Studies

    2. Master of Afro-American Studies

    3. Ph.D. of Afro-American Studies

6. The instructors will be of the Black Experience.

The reason the proposal are revolutionary are:

A. It would be the first Afro American College on a white campus anywhere in the world.

B. It would be received as an "act of good faith" if implemented as proposed and only as proposed. We ask no more, will accept no less.

C. There is absolutely no reason why it cannot be done.

However we need the support of all the people: the support of Black people in the U.S. and throughout the world.

This support is needed on two ways from all the people; financial and written.

In short, we need any type of financial and/or public expression we can receive: Papers, periodicals, TV, Radio, speeches, etc.

We will send spokesmen anywhere to discuss and speak on this subject at your convenience.

The Black Liberation Movement can be contacted by writing:

The Black Liberation Movement

P.O. Box 1502
Santa Cruz, California 95060

"Yours in Freedom."
The Black Liberation Movement

Notes

1   "Revolutionary intercommunalism" is a Marxist-Leninist inspired analytic framework. Newton used this to interpret. and in turn. combat the subordination of the black community to the market needs of the white economic elite. The analysis goes further in that it recognizes that the world has reached a highly developed technological state in which thinking in terms of national borders (and mentalities) or international inter-relations is obsolete. The fact that we have a small world community today, "... means that a new revolutionary spirit can count on a common technology and communication, a joint fund of information and education, all transcending mutual nationalist isolation and corporate structures of their individual societies" (*In Search of Common Ground*, p. 58). What we now have is a highly developed, technological world community in which U.S. imperialism plays the role of a white economic elite and saps off the resources and strength of Jess powerful nations. Central to revolutionary intercommunalism is the belief "that everything is in a constant state of transformation" thus differentiating the BPP from other civil/human rights organizations in that "... these principles ... (gave the BPP)... an ability to grow through self-criticism" (*War Against the Panthers*, p.35). The present political situation is that of bourgeois capitalism, which for all intents and purposes is the same as fascism for blacks in America (*To Die for The People*, p. 58).

2   Party members would tail police to the scene of the "crime" and then, at a legally approved distance, inform the alleged "criminal" of his/her constitutional rights (*War Against the Panthers*, p.38).

3   The Mulford Act was a law passed by the California State Legislature that required a licence to carry a firearm. Previous-

ly, the law stated that the carrying of arms was perfectly legal so long as they were not concealed. The right to bear arms was revoked on account of Black Panther Party members carrying unconcealed, loaded firearms. This brings up the question of whether blacks really do have the same rights as whites (or at least the same protection). Never before had this constitutional right been questioned before black people decided to exercise it. This is verified by the fact that the law was quite often and openly referred to as the "Panther Bill" by the media (*War Against the Panthers*, p.41).

4   The COINTELPRO assassination of Hampton and Mark Clark was considered successful by FBI officials. Four days later, the raiders were applauded by state attorney Hanrahan for exercising professional restraint in not killing everyone at the residence. Close ties with the Chicago Tribune allowed the FBI to place its version of the incident in the media. Likewise, CBS led an FBI supervised re-enactment of the raid (*Agents of Repression*, p.71-73). Only later were the true facts of the raid known. Hampton and Clark had been slaughtered in cold blood.

5   In *Revolutionary Suicide*, Newton writes that to be a true revolutionary one has to accept their death, in fact, must realize that they are already dead. But this is not a call by Newton to his foUowers to meaninglessly sacrifice themselves as some academics have suggested. Rather, in the spirit of revolutionary struggles, it calls for men and women to move to "... wipe out the overwhelming force of an oppressive army" at any cost, not simply to put a gun to their head and pull the trigger, which is "reactionary suicide" (p.6). On page 15 of *Insights and Poems*, a collaboration with Erika Huggens, Newton contemplated the concept,

> By having no family
> I inherited the family of humanity.

By having no possessions
I have possessed all.
By rejecting the love of one
I received the love of all.
By surrendering my life to the revolution
I found eternal life.
Revolutionary Suicide.

6   Governor Ronald Reagan proposed these limits on facuity to be affimed by the UCRegents:

A. Faculty cannot govern the university, a right reserved by the Regents.
B. Faculty are not allowed to authorize and supervise courses, except by specific rule of the Regents.
C. Only Regent's can award degrees.
D. Faculty appointments to made by the Regents, president and chancellor of the university.
E. UCB board that approved the Cleaver course disallowed to create new courses.

Luckily, the Regents overturned his proposal (*City on a Hill*, "Reagan confrontation with students materializes at Regent's meeting," 10/25/68).

7   8   12 Lease, a notorious pig-not police-but boar hunter is now being considered for dismissal on charges of sexually harrassing a prospective female professor during an interview. Many faculty objected to his characterization of Newton during their interviews with me. Trivers said, "I knew them well and I never thought that she ... was treated in a disrespectful way as a bauble ... if I brought my wife into a class ... she might very well sit in the back by her own choice." Noel King also contradicted Lease's description of Newton, believing his work with universal identity was a definite indication of his egalitarian conception of sexual roles. Likewise, all of Newton's professional writings speak to the need for equal

rights for women.

9   The car White refers to had been a gift from Bert Schneider. As for the suit, it was Newton's BPP uniform. He actually wore a ceramic military-style band on his chest made for him by Lee's wife, Charlene.

10   Newton is continually referred to in many articles as an ex-felon, when in fact his status as such was unclear. Newton's attorney, Floyd Silliman, tried to block the charges that Newton was an ex-felon in possession of a weapon, because the 1964 conviction of assault against Newton had been overturned by an Alameda Superior Court because he had not been properly advised to his right of counsel (7/14/78).

11   That there could be any confusion between the two men is ludicrous as Newton stood but six-feet and weighed 150 pounds, while Robert Heard was seven-feet and at least twice Newtons· weight.

12   (same as 7)

13   Reverend Herb Schmidt, the first campus paster at UCSC, old me that Newton had contacted him in 1980, voicing his desire to become ordained into the Lutheran ministry. Schmidt proceeded to check with national church authorities and it was impossible to arrange. Schmidt was very supportive and willing to help Newton, but Newton was unwilling to pass through all of the institutional hoops required by the ordaining process.

14   It should be mentioned that Edgar Hoover's COINTELPRO agenda included an active role to "prevent the coalition of militant black nationalist groups ... prevent them from gaining respectability ... Prevent the rise of a black 'messiah' who would unify, electrify, the militant black nationalist movement. Malcomb X (sic) might have been such a 'messiah'" (*Agents of Repression*. p. 58)

CPSIA information can be obtained
at www.ICGtesting.com
Printed in the USA
JSHW011731280323
39571JS00002B/96